Gold
From
Dark
Mines

Gold
From
Dark Mines

Providence and grace in the lives
of six famous Christians

Irene Howat

CHRISTIAN FOCUS

© Copyright Christian Focus Publications Ltd.

ISBN 1-85792-943-8

10 9 8 7 6 5 4 3 2 1

Published in 2005
by
Christian Focus Publications, Ltd.,
Geanies House, Fearn, Tain,
Ross-shire, IV20 1TW, Scotland

www.christianfocus.com

Printed and bound by
Nørhaven Paperback A/S, Denmark

Cover Design by Alister MacInnes

Contents

1

Of Providence and Grace

All who are born into this world are citizens of the world by virtue of their very existence. However, that does not automatically make them citizens of heaven hereafter. Nicodemus, a member of the ruling council in Jerusalem in Jesus' day, was an open-minded man. He had heard what Jesus was teaching and doing and wanted to know whether his authority came from God or if he was a charlatan. Although the question he asked the Lord relates to authority, in his reply Jesus told Nicodemus how a citizen of the world becomes a citizen of heaven.

'Now there was a man of the Pharisees named Nicodemus, a member of the Jewish ruling council. He came to Jesus at night and said, "Rabbi, we know you are a teacher who has come from God. For no-one could perform the miraculous signs you are doing if God were not with him." In reply Jesus declared, "I tell you the truth, no one can see the kingdom of God unless he is born again.[" "How can a man be born when he is old?" Nicodemus asked. "Surely he cannot enter a second time into

his mother's womb to be born!" Jesus answered, "I tell you the truth, no one can enter the kingdom of God unless he is born of water and the Spirit. Flesh gives birth to flesh, but the Spirit gives birth to spirit. You should not be surprised at my saying, "You must be born again." The wind blows wherever it pleases. You hear its sound, but you cannot tell where it comes from or where it is going. So it is with everyone born of the Spirit. … Just as Moses lifted up the snake in the desert, so the Son of Man must be lifted up, that everyone who believes in him may have eternal life. For God so loved the world that he gave his one and only Son, that whoever believes in him shall not perish but have eternal life".

John 3:1-8, 14-16

Birth and Rebirth

Jesus' words show quite clearly that just as there needs to be birth into this world, there needs to be rebirth into the kingdom of heaven. Christians are those who are born again. It is interesting to note that although the Lord stresses the necessity of rebirth he does not describe the process. And the New Testament makes it clear that the process is as varied as the people concerned. Saul (who became Paul) was born again when he met the Lord in a dramatic encounter as he travelled towards Damascus to hound believers there. The change in him was immediate (Acts 9:1-19). Some people in Berea heard Paul and Silas preaching. They listened carefully then searched through the Old Testament to discover if what they were hearing accorded with what was prophesied. Finding that it did, they continued to listen to the apostles preaching until eventually they were born again (Acts 17:10-12). The Ethiopian Eunuch was born again when a passage in Isaiah was explained to him (Acts 8:26-40). What these people had in common was that they came to a saving faith in Jesus – they were born again – but each had a different experience of rebirth.

One danger into which parts of the church have fallen at various times in its history is that they created formulae for becoming a Christian that were so tight that people often could not fit their experience into them. And the same is true today. Some groups have a formula for conversion that they treat as a pattern to which people must conform before being accepted into membership. They must have experience A, followed by experience B, followed by experience C. Anything else is too loose, and variation of order or form raises doubts about authenticity. But the Holy Spirit will not be constrained by our formulae. Jesus does not provide a checklist of sixteen points to be gone through in the correct order so that it can be signed, dated and stamped at the bottom as some kind of passport to heaven. He said, 'Unless a man is born again, he cannot see the kingdom of God.'

What does the Bible say about the new birth? Paul wrote, 'We ought always to thank God for you, brothers loved by the Lord, because from the beginning God chose you to be saved through the sanctifying work of the Spirit and through belief in the truth' (2 Thess. 2:13). The origin of a Christian's rebirth is in heaven 'before the beginning' when God chose him to be his own. Those whom God has chosen since before the beginning of time will hear his call, will answer it through the gift of faith that he gives them and will be reborn as children of God. Not only that, but their citizenship in heaven is secure thereafter.

> 'Who shall separate us from the love of Christ? Shall trouble or hardship or persecution or famine or nakedness or danger or sword? As it is written: "For your sake we face death all day long; we are considered as sheep to be slaughtered." No, in all these things we are more than conquerors through him who loved us. For I am convinced that neither death nor life, neither angels nor demons, neither the present nor the future, nor any powers, neither height nor depth, nor anything else in all creation, will be able to separate us from the love of God that is in Christ Jesus our Lord'.
>
> Romans 8:35-39

Six Examples from History

Many Christian biographies begin with accounts of rebirth then tell what happen thereafter. Little attention is sometimes paid to the years before conversion. The emphasis of this book is a little different. As God has chosen his people from before the beginning of time, his interest in them does not start at their conversion. David recognised that.

> *'You created my inmost being; you knit me together in my mother's womb. I praise you because I am fearfully and wonderfully made; your works are wonderful, I know that full well. My frame was not hidden from you when I was made in the secret place. When I was woven together in the depths of the earth, your eyes saw my unformed body. All the days ordained for me were written in your book before one of them came to be.'* No wonder he went on to say, *'How precious to me are your thoughts, O God! How vast is the sum of them!'*
>
> Psalm 139:13-17

David knew that God's interest in him and involvement with him extended back to before he was born, and Christians know that God's interest in them stretches back to eternity, and certainly includes the years before they were reborn. They may seem like lost years, but the Lord not only redeems his people's souls, he redeems their experiences too. What is experienced and learned in the 'lost' years is put to use in the kingdom's work. Gold from Dark Mines focuses on the pre-conversion years of its six subjects and how they came to faith. It goes on to tell their life stories in brief before concluding each one by illustrating how God used the experiences they went through before conversion to his glory. It aims to show God's providential dealings with his chosen children before his work of grace took place in their hearts, and how in his good providence he redeemed their lost years by turning them into tools they could use to help in the great work of building his kingdom and preparing for the King of kings to come in glory.

Charles Spurgeon wrote, 'True seekers will hunt everywhere for Jesus, and will not be too proud to learn from beggars and little children. We take gold from dark mines and muddy streams …' It is surely true that the darkest mine from which believers take spiritual gold is the dark mine of their own pre-conversion experience. How good God is to use the lost years.

2

Augustine of Hippo

Souk Ahras in modern Algeria was the birthplace of the child who was to become probably the greatest Father of the Christian church. In 354 AD, Algeria was Numidia, the town of Thagaste stood where Souk Ahras now stands, and it was ruled from Rome, as was most of the known world. Augustine's parents were typical of the time and place. Monica was a Christian and Patricius a pagan who worshipped the Roman gods. He seems to have been tolerant of his wife's faith. She, believing her husband to be her master, did what pleased him and created a peaceable home. Monica's view of the marriage relationship allowed her to accept Patricius's infidelities without becoming a quarrelsome and bitter wife. It was to this long-suffering young woman and her occasionally hot-headed and philandering husband that Augustine was born. 1600 years after the event we know that the infant smiled in his sleep before he smiled awake! Augustine in his Confessions records that his mother told him so.

There is a tenderness in the telling of such things and a love in the remembering of them. Young Augustine was loved and he knew it.

Tracing Augustine's spiritual journey so many hundreds of years later is possible because he recorded it in his Confessions. As a small child at school we find him praying that the Lord would remove the consequences of his sin, that he would not be flogged by his schoolmaster for preferring kicking a ball around to doing his lessons. Monica had taught him well, but in praying for the avoidance of sin's consequences rather than for forgiveness we see that his childhood theology was anything but sound. Even as a child, Augustine applied his critical faculties to what was happening around him. 'The trifling occupations of older people are called "business"; but those of boys... are punished by those elders.'

Such a perceptive boy must have been aware very early of the difference in his parents' beliefs. His father, the only member of the household who was not a Christian, did not force his pagan beliefs on his son. The fact that Patricius's servants were Christians speaks of his tolerance. He did not, says Augustine, 'prevail over the power of my mother's piety in me, that I should believe in Christ the less, because he did not yet believe.' The man's tolerance must have been strained to the limit when, still a boy, Augustine took seriously ill. Thinking he might die, the lad asked his mother to arrange for his immediate baptism. That put her in a quandary. If her son was indeed dying she wanted him baptised right away. But, if he was going to survive, her will was to delay baptism because she believed that sins committed after the sacrament had been administered would be more severely dealt with than those committed before. And she knew her son. The crisis passed and baptism was deferred.

School was the cause of much rebellion on the part of the growing Augustine. It was only years later that he began to appreciate the efforts of those who had forced him to knuckle down and get on with his work. Greek was a particular hatred of his, though he loved the study of Latin. That opened up a world of books that a boy of his age and temperament most appreciated. There were battle strategies to come to grips with and romances to enjoy. Unfortunately there was also a plethora of stories of immoral deities, stories he and his father probably shared together as they involved the gods in whom Patricius believed. How his mother must have prayed as she saw her son enticed away from what she had taught him of the Lord.

Years later Augustine looked back on his teenage years and described his young self. '…

I was offensive even to such as myself... with innumerable lies deceiving my tutor, my masters, my parents, from love of play, eagerness to see vain shows and restlessness to imitate stage plays… Thefts I also committed from my parents' cellar and table, either because tempted by gluttony, or that I might have to give to boys, who sold me their play, which all the while they delighted in as much as I did. In this play, too, I often sought to win by cheating; won over myself meanwhile by coveting to excel.' Not only that but he was hypocritical with it, because he goes on, 'What could I so ill put up with, or, when I found it out, did I denounce so fiercely, as that very thing which I was doing to others, and for which, found out, I was denounced, but yet chose rather to quarrel than to yield.' His hypocrisy seems to have been a passing phase because before long we find him 'delighting' in truth, and taking great offence when he was deceived.

Monica's heart no doubt was sore as she watched her son travel through his sixteenth year, and it may be that Patricius took delight in what saddened his wife. Having fed his mind on the immoral doings of the Roman gods the hormone-driven youth could not distinguish love from lust and he entered into relationships about which he was to become heartily ashamed. 'In that sixteenth year of the age of my flesh, in the madness of lust which hath license through men's viciousness … I resigned myself wholly to it. My friends meanwhile took no care by marriage to save me from ruin; their only care was that I should learn to make a good speech, and be a persuasive orator.'

A 4th Century Gap Year

It was at this point that Augustine took what is now known as a gap year. Having finished school he stayed at home for a year during which money was to be raised for his further education. His intellectual ability had been recognised, but his father, 'a poor freedman of Thagaste', was not able to fund studies in Carthage immediately. A youth from Augustine's social group would not have expected great efforts to be made to fund his education, but Patricius was determined to do just that. Years later Augustine noted that although his father was prepared to do all he could to secure his son's education he wasn't in the least concerned about his immoral and chaotic lifestyle. If fact, Patricius seemed to have taken delight in his masculinity and interest in the opposite sex. Once, having seen Augustine undressed at the public baths, he rushed home and told his wife that he thought they would soon be grandparents! It appears that Patricius was beginning to show some interest in the Christian faith because it is recorded that he had become a catechumen, though his thinking on morality seems still to have been unchanged. That was in stark contrast to Monica who was 'startled with a holy fear and trembling.' So urgent was her concern that she took Augustine aside and warned him against the sin of fornication, especially where it involved a married woman.

His mother's words fell on deaf ears, but Monica knew her prayers were heard and she waited for them to be answered. Her faith was founded on the Lord for it most certainly wasn't founded on her son. Augustine needed to be one up on his friends. If they boasted he found something greater to boast about, even if it was fictitious. Not only did he live to excess, he needed to know that he was in excess of his friends as regards his vices. His gap year turned out to be a nightmare for his mother as he careered further and further from the faith in which she had nurtured him, and appeared to be racing headlong towards hell. Having said that, Monica did not advise Augustine to marry rather than live immorally with his mistress because she thought that an early marriage might hamper his future prospects.

It was about this time that the teenaged Augustine indulged in a senseless act of vandalism for no reason other than to express 'a loathing of righteousness and a surfeit of iniquity.' On seeing a pear tree laden with fruit, he and a group of his friends stripped it of its pears and threw them to some nearby pigs. In a younger child this might have been a game of daring carried too far in the excitement of the moment. But that was not the case for Augustine. It was an act of open rebellion against the Lord. He had reached a state of hating all that his mother had taught him and there was something in the wantonness of the destruction that made it an expression of that hatred. He satisfied his lust because he wanted to. He lied because he wanted to. But he didn't want the inferior pears. There was 'no temptation to that evil deed, but the evil deed itself.'

Perhaps even Patricius heaved a sigh of relief when Augustine left for Carthage to further his studies. The opportunity for a new start was stillborn and the youth took up in Carthage where he had left off in Thagaste. Of his early months in Carthage Augustine wrote, 'Within me was a famine of that inward food, Thyself, my God; yet, through that famine I was not hungered; but was without all longing for incorruptible sustenance, not because filled therewith, but the more empty, the more I loathed it.' His conduct had stifled the least desire for the Lord, and that being stifled he had grown to loathe everything that it stood for. Yet, despite all he did to avoid it there was sadness in his life, a sadness that he nurtured by going to plays full of pathos. But it was a second-hand sadness, allowing him to grieve for what was unreal while he ignored the reality of his sinfulness. It might be thought that such a young man would never be seen in a place of worship. That was not the case, but whatever took Augustine to 'the celebration of Thy solemnities, within the walls of Thy church,' what happened when he was there was disgraceful, 'deserving death for its fruits.' One of the fruits of his dissolute behaviour was that Augustine contracted a 'foul disease'.

Not withstanding the young man's extra-curricular activities, Augustine shone at his studies and was soon chief in the School of Rhetoric, and proud he was of it. No doubt his father would also have been proud, but it seems that the man who scrimped and saved to send his son to university did not live to see the fruits of his success. Augustine recorded this in the most offhand way. When writing about his financial situation, he adds, in parenthesis, 'my father being dead two years before.' Nineteen years old he seemed to have thrown over the traces completely. But, when required to study Cicero, there grew in Augustine a desire for wisdom. It was then that his early teaching crept back into his mind, that wisdom came from God. The only thing he could see that was missing from Cicero's thinking on the subject was Christ. It would have delighted his mother to see him beginning to study his Bible in his search for wisdom. No doubt she was praying for him, for all his years were blessed with his mother's prayers, even the most wayward years of his life. But it was not yet time for her prayers to be answered. Augustine's reaction to God's Word was one of disdain. It contained none of Cicero's lofty language and seemed to him altogether less dignified, as though he would have to lower himself to understand it. In other words, he recognised the need for a humble approach to the Bible, but that was not his approach.

It was then that Augustine took up with the Manichees who believed a hotch-potch 'theology' derived from Christianity, Judaism, philosophy and superstition that seemed to give them the answers to all their questions. And when a question arose for which they didn't have an answer they tacked on something else to their eclectic collection of beliefs. Augustine felt at home with them. Imagine how Monica reacted when she arrived in Carthage to make a home there for herself. Having prayed for her son's conversion, she found him an out-and-out heretic, so much so that it seems she banned him from eating at her table! Not only was Monica a woman who prayed tenaciously, she was also quite able to put her son in his place, for all the exalted position he now held among the intelligentsia of Carthage.

Doing what she did best, Monica resorted to more prayer. She must have been the embodiment of 'praying continually' (1 Thess. 5:17). When he wrote his Confessions, Augustine records, 'my mother, the faithful one, wept for me to Thee, more than mothers weep for the death of children's bodies … Thou heardest her, and despised not her tears, when streaming forth, they watered the earth beneath her eyes in every place of her prayer.' God answered Monica with a dream in which she was assured that one day she and Augustine would stand side by side in the faith. So conceited was her son that when she told him of her dream he assumed that she was going to espouse his heretical thinking! She was not amused. Even at the time Monica's reaction impressed the young man.

In an effort to hasten on God's answer to her prayers Monica approached one of the bishops in Carthage, asking him to talk to Augustine and to refute his errors, 'unteach him' what he believed and instruct him in the truth. The bishop was in the habit of approaching people in this way, but he recognised that Augustine was too proud to be teachable. Explaining that he too had been captivated by Manicheism in his youth, the wise man advised Monica to, 'let him alone for a while. Only pray God for him.' That did not satisfy the anxious woman and she pressed him further, weeping as she did so. 'Go thy ways,' the Bishop told her, 'and God be with you; it is not possible that the son of these tears should perish.' His words spoke to Monica like a voice from heaven and she clung to them in the years that followed.

The life Augustine lived might today be described as cultic, so engaged was he in the practices of the Manichees. How else could one describe such gross excesses as 'desiring to be cleansed from … defilements, by carrying food to those who were called "elect" and "saints," out of which, in the workshop of their stomachs, they should forge for us angels and gods, by whom we might be delivered.' But there were boundaries beyond which even he would not go. When a wizard offered to help Augustine win a verse competition he gave him very short shrift. And there was a stability in his life that had not been there before. Although not married, he had found a woman with whom he could live in a loving rather than a lustful relationship. Not only that, but 'he was faithful to her bed'. Although the irregularity of that relationship must have distressed his mother, she could not but be relieved that it had curbed his former excesses. His faithfulness to his mistress was for the girl's sake rather than because of any Christian sense of right and wrong. He certainly had no time for biblical teaching against the occult as was evidenced by his fascination with astrology as a means of divining the future. Augustine was quite addicted to it, every bit as much as those who rely of horoscopes today. Even Vindicianus, a man whose wisdom he admired, and his dear friend Nebridius could not wean him off it.

Having been singularly successful as a student and a teacher in Carthage, and having made quite a name for himself in academic circles, Augustine returned to Thagaste as a schoolmaster. There he picked up a friendship from childhood. Before long his friend began to be persuaded of Augustine's heretical teachings. Devoted to each other, the two men spent many hours discussing and debating. His friend's Christian leanings were soon discarded as Augustine pressed his Manichean thinking upon him. Then a day came when his friend 'sore sick of a fever … lay insensible in a death-sweat'. With hope of his survival gone, the young man's family had him baptised. Much to everyone's surprise he rallied and seemed set to recover. As soon as possible thereafter – and it was very soon – Augustine made a joke about baptism doing any good especially when the person being baptised was soundly unconscious. Expecting his friend to scoff with him, he was more than a little taken aback when he was told to stop saying such things if he wished to remain a friend. Augustine decided to leave the matter until the patient was stronger, then to 'deal with him'. It was not to be. A few days later the young man's fever returned and he died.

Such was the friendship they had enjoyed that Augustine was overwhelmed with grief. 'Whatever I had shared with him, for lack of him became a ghastly torture.' Grief produced a mixed reaction in the young man. While a great weariness of life afflicted him, he was at the same time plagued by a fear of death. Although he tried to cast his burden on his mother's God, he admitted that to him God was neither real nor substantial. So it is little wonder that his burden 'glided though the void, and fell down again on (him).' Unable to escape his grief, Augustine decided to escape Thagaste and return to Carthage and his friends there. While his mind could engage in serious and deep study it baulked at death. And by way of coping he threw himself into work, writing two or three books on 'the fair and the fit'. The fair he defined as that which had an intrinsic beauty and the fit was that which had its beauty in how it related to other things. Those books, now lost, doubtless reflected the Manichean soup in which he continued to swim.

Not Ignorant of Ignorance

As he reached the end of his twenties, Augustine had the opportunity to meet Faustus, a Manichean bishop. The man had a reputation for being charming and erudite and his young follower looked forward to hearing him. But although he praised the bishop, Augustine was able to distinguish the truth he sought from what he heard expounded. Employing a splendid turn of phrase regarding Faustus's eruditeness and the content of what he said, Augustine wrote, 'Nor did I care so much how that Faustus … dished up his discourse, as what kind of food of knowledge he set before me.' While the presentation was good the content left the hungry man empty. Determined to discuss things at depth with Faustus, Augustine grasped the opportunity when it came his way. The exchange was most unsatisfactory for both of them. The bishop was totally outclassed by the seeker and the seeker left with his questions unanswered. 'It became clear to me,' Augustine concluded, 'that he was ignorant of those arts in which I had thought he excelled, I began to despair of his opening and solving the difficulties which perplexed me …' Then cryptically he added, 'he was not altogether ignorant of his own ignorance, and did not choose to be caught in a dispute …' Fautus' modesty or wiliness appealed to Augustine, but what he said did not. His mother's prayers were beginning to be answered as her son lost faith in the Manichean teaching. And having turned his back on it he looked around for what to do and where to go. That was when the thought of Rome grew in its appeal to him.

Carthage in the 380s was an ill-disciplined place. Students took up subjects and dropped them on a whim, and they did the same with teachers. Not only that, they interrupted lectures and distracted those who were serious about their studies. Although he had lived a chaotic life himself that kind of behaviour did not appeal to Augustine at all. Having heard that students in Rome took their studies seriously, that they were restrained and disciplined, and that his salary there would be more than in Carthage, he decided to cross the Mediterranean Sea and head for the capital of the Empire. Arrangements were made for his move, and the time came for Augustine to travel north to the coast where he would find a ship sailing for Italy. Monica had other ideas. Not only did she object to his going to Rome, she followed him right to the Mediterranean coast, clinging to her son either to stop him leaving or to demand that she went with him. He would have none of it. Lying to his mother, he persuaded her to stay the night at a place right beside where his ship was berthed. Leaving her weeping and praying, he assured her he would see her in the morning. By the time she was on the quayside the next morning – and doubtless it was early – her son was at sea. 'She loved my being with her, as mothers do' Augustine remembered, then added, 'but much more than many. … I cannot express the affection she bare to me, and with how much more vehement anguish she was now in labour of me in the spirit, than when she bare me in the flesh.'

He had escaped from his mother, but Augustine could not escape from her prayers. And that was just as well, for no sooner had he arrived in Rome than he went down with a life-threatening fever. Despite knowing he might die, Augustine had the integrity not to call for baptism. He was not a belts and braces man. What he believed, he believed, and he would not compromise even on what he thought might be his deathbed. He did, however, recover. Having taken ill in the house of a Manichee he aligned himself once again with the sect when he was fit to do so, but he was not in great sympathy with their teaching. He found his mind straying towards the Bible, but there was one huge stumbling block. Augustine was unable to accept that Jesus could have been born of Mary without his deity being contaminated by his intimate contact with her. However, he was open-minded and honest enough to recognise that his Manichean reservations regarding the Bible were not all well-founded. The whole issue became oppressive to him. His humour was not improved when he discovered that although Roman students were not as rowdy as those in Carthage, they were a dishonest lot. It was their custom to attend a teacher's house to benefit from his learning, then to conspire together to move on just before their accounts were due to be paid!

Bishop Ambrose

Word came to Rome from Milan requesting that a teacher of rhetoric be sent there. Having had his fill of his Roman students Augustine was not slow to apply for the position. He was examined, found suitable, and sent at the public expense to Milan. In Milan at that time was the man God had appointed to reach out to Augustine. He was Bishop Ambrose, 'known to the whole world as among the best of men.' Later Augustine put it beautifully, 'To him (Ambrose) I was unknowingly led by Thee, that by him I might knowingly be led to Thee.' But that was a little while in the future. Augustine's first impression of Ambrose was of a good-hearted, generous and hospitable man with whom he could engage. Having lost his father when he was seventeen years old, he found a father figure in the bishop. His speech was less sparkling than that of Faustus, but his content was deeper. Augustine listened diligently to him preaching to the people though he freely admitted that he appreciated his eloquence rather than the substance of his sermons. So he was able to comment that, 'I hung on his words attentively; but with regard to the matter was but a careless and scornful bystander.'

By the time Augustine reached Milan he had virtually given up hope of finding the truth or of there being a specific truth to find. Consequently, it must have come as a surprise to him that as he listened to Ambrose's words for the words' sake, he found himself considering what he had for years turned his back upon. Somehow these two could not be separated in his mind. When admitting that the bishop spoke eloquently, something in Augustine, and that something increased with time, wanted to add that he also spoke truly. For the first time since he was a boy he began to question if his mother's gospel was capable of defence. In the course of his preaching Ambrose tackled some Old Testament passages that had been stumbling blocks to Augustine. Being a man of intellectual integrity, the young man set out to see if he could convict the Manichees of falsehood. Finding that he could, he loosed himself from the sect completely and became a Catechumen (one under instruction) in the Christian faith. Honesty did not allow him to commit himself, but he was prepared to go that far. There is an interesting snippet at this point of his Confessions. 'I determined therefore so long to be a Catechumen in the Catholic Church, to which I had been commended by my parents, till something certain should dawn upon me, whither I might direct my course.' It is easy to read into his early years that only Monica encouraged him in Christian things, but it seems from his use of 'parents' here that his father, whom we last hear of as a Catechumen, did perhaps come to faith in Christ before his early death.

Milan was not too far for the intrepid Monica to travel to see her son again. Promising the sailors a safe arrival because she believed it was God's will that she go to Augustine, she comforted them when the seas were rough. Augustine was not in the best of spirits when she arrived; nor was his mother as overjoyed when she heard that he had left Manicheism as he had expected her to be. Relieved, as she no doubt was about that, what she was interested in was his conversion and nothing short of it. His condition only inspired her to 'pour forth more copious prayers and tears.'

Augustine said that, 'She believed in Christ, and before she departed out of this life, she should see me a faithful Catholic.' It has to be remembered that the word Catholic in the sense in which he used it refers to the church universal rather than the Roman Catholic Church. Monica's prayer was that her son would be part of the church universal, the body of Christ on earth.

An incident occurred not long after Monica's arrival in Milan that caused her son to pause for thought. At home in Thagaste she had been in the habit of presenting things to the saints and leaving her offerings to them on their memorials. When she tried to do that in Milan the doorkeeper forbade her. Making it her business to find out why, Monica soon discovered that the bishop had forbidden the practice. 'She piously and obediently embraced his wishes' and Augustine 'wondered at how readily she censured her own practice, rather than dispute his prohibition.' It seems that the practice had descended into an alcoholic binge for some who took part in it as wine was drunk at every memorial and there was a great number of them. In fact, Monica carried the same small cup of wine, well diluted with water, from memorial to memorial and was as sober at the end of her act of piety as at the beginning. Realising the wisdom of Ambrose's thinking, and accepting that taking part could lead some into excess, she bowed to his decision without complaint. Her attitude to this made a great impression on her son. It also made an impression on Ambrose who told Augustine what a fine and pious mother he had, little knowing what a wayward and rebellious son she had endured.

Soul-searching

Meanwhile Augustine watched the bishop carefully and tested all that he said. He longed to discuss in depth with Ambrose, but the bishop always seemed to be surrounded by people needing his advice and pastoral care. On those occasions when he did come upon Ambrose alone he found him deep in a book and could not disturb him. By then Augustine attended church every Lord's Day and listened to what Ambrose taught. There followed a period of soul-searching which revealed things that disturbed the Catechumen. 'So rash and impious had I been, that what I ought to have said in the way of enquiry, I had said in the way of condemnation.' The reader of his Confessions notes the beginning of a more humble approach to his search for truth. Of course, one of the things he discovered when his pride began to go was that whether or not the Church taught the truth it certainly did not teach the things which for years he had condemned it. Augustine's learned mind was discovering the extent of its own ignorance. Later he wrote of this period of his life, 'As it happens that one, who has tried a bad physician, fears to trust himself to a good one, so was it with the health of my soul, which could not be healed but by believing, and for fear of believing falsehoods, refused to be cured; resisting Thy hands, who has prepared the medicines of faith …' Before long he was able to say that he believed that God was, and that God cared. Progress indeed.

Living in Milan at the same time as Augustine were two of his friends, Alypius and Nebridius. Alypius, who was some years younger than Augustine, was also from Thagaste. Not only that, but he had studied under him both in their home town and in Carthage. However, in Milan Alypius was more interested in the circus than in sitting under his old master. We have to remember that the circus was not a matter of clowns and high-wire acts; it was deadly serious sport, quite literally, for it sometimes ended in the deaths of the contestants. Although that concerned Augustine, he had not broached the subject with his young friend. However, one day Alypius joined Augustine's scholars, just as the master quoted the circus as an example of what he was saying. God used the words of the still unbelieving rhetorician to speak to the young man's heart. Soon Alypius was numbered among Augustine's scholars. The pair were seeking for truth, as was their friend Nebridius, and they sought it together.

Although Augustine lived with his mistress they remained unmarried. They did have a son together whom his father loved deeply. Monica, ever seeking the best for Augustine, prevailed on him to find a wife – not to marry his mistress. A girl was found, though she was two years short of marriageable age, and it was decided that the time had come for him to part with the love of his youth. It was not a happy parting. 'My mistress being torn from my side as a hindrance to my marriage, my heart which clave unto her was torn and wounded and bleeding. And she returned to Africa, vowing unto Thee never to know any other man, leaving me with my son by her.' Augustine was right when he said, 'my sins were being multiplied' for he took another woman as his mistress for the two years before his marriage was due to take place. Little wonder he recorded that he became more miserable with the passage of time. Although he sought God he certainly was not honouring him in his life. His comfort was to be found in discussions with Alypius and Nebridius.

The subjects they studied at depth were deep indeed. Was God corruptible? Stemmed from Augustine's earlier problem about Jesus being defiled through having been born to an ordinary human mother. Was the freedom of the will the cause of all evil? If God is the sovereign good, can he then be considered as the cause of evil? Although these discussions often had no end, one thing had ended and that was Augustine's fascination with astrology. To put it in his own strong words, 'I had rejected the lying divinations and impious ravings of the astrologers.' By then he had a core of belief to which he held: that God existed, that he was unchanging and unchangeable, that he exercised providence and judgement upon men, and that in Christ – whom he believed to be God's son and the Lord of believers – and in the scriptures, which the Church had made binding and that God had appointed a way of salvation to life after this life. Augustine had come a long way in his thinking, but he was not yet where his mother prayed him to be. The question of the origin of evil perplexed him terribly and became a stumbling block to his understanding. Once again, it was when he realised that he was pitting his intellect against the Word of God that he was humbled enough to move further towards the truth. The period that followed was one of discovery. As he applied his mind humbly to the matter his misted understanding began to clear.

From time to time Augustine was surprised by a joy that could only have come from the Lord. 'I was amazed that I now loved Thee, and no phantasm instead of thee,' he wrote. And the search went on. 'I continued to seek for a way of gaining strength which should enable me to enjoy Thee ... for not yet did I cling to Jesus.' Monica, aware of her son's spiritual warfare, no doubt redoubled her efforts in prayer. Alongside his Bible Augustine often had some Platonist books and he compared the two. As his search went on those books satisfied him less and God's Word drew him more. Not only that, his humbled state of mind allowed him to take his troubles to an older and wise Christian. His name was Simplicianus. As Ambrose seemed a father figure to Augustine (though they were only fourteen years apart in age) so Simplicianus was a father figure to the bishop. The seeker poured out his heart to his mentor, mentioning in the passing Victorinus, formerly a professor of rhetoric in Rome. Immediately Simplicianus's eyes lit up and he told Augustine how, before he died, that pagan professor had 'pronounced the true faith with an excellent boldness.' How Augustine 'burned to imitate him', but still he held back.

One day, when Augustine and Alypius were together, a Christian visited and shared his testimony with them. It had a profound effect on the older man. 'Such was the story of Pontitianus; but Thou, O Lord, while he was speaking, didst turn me round towards myself, taking me from behind my back where I had placed me, unwilling of observing myself, and setting me before my face, that I might see how foul I was, how crooked and defiled, bespotted and ulcerous.' Augustine was under conviction of sin. Into his mind came a prayer he had uttered in his early youth, 'Give me chastity and continency, only not yet.' With appalling clarity he recognised that the time had come when he was to see himself for the wretch he was. His arguments against the Christian faith, he realised, had reached an end of themselves and all that was left was a dreadful fear of the implications of the life he had led.

In the Garden

That was Augustine's state of mind and heart when he met Alypius and the pair went through their lodging into the garden at the rear. Augustine, going as far from the house as possible was in an agony of body and soul. Sin was pressing down on him fearfully. Alypius watched and listened as his master and friend was brought to his lowest point.

'How long, Lord, wilt Thou be angry, for ever?' he heard him weep, then, 'Why not now? Why not this hour make an end of my uncleanness?' From the garden of the neighbouring house came a young boy's voice, one that could not have contrasted more strongly with Augustine's. 'Take, read; take, read,' chanted the childish voice. The words broke through Augustine's torment and he found himself wondering if these were the words of a game he didn't know. Discounting that, he took them to be a divine command. Paul's letter to the Romans was there in front of him, and taking it in his hands he opened and read what was in front of his eyes. Alypius watched and listened as his friend read. 'Not in rioting and drunkenness, not in chambering and wantonness, not in strife and envying: but put ye on the Lord Jesus Christ, and make not provision for the flesh to fulfil the lusts thereof' (Rom. 13:13-14 KJV). Peace flooded his heart and all shadow of doubt melted away.

What happened next should be left to Augustine to tell, for it concerns Monica who had prayed for that moment probably from before her son was born. 'Thence we go in to my mother; we tell her; she rejoiceth: we relate in order how it took place; she exulteth, and triumpheth, and blessed Thee, "Who are able to do above than which we ask or think" (Eph. 3:20); for she perceived that Thou hadst given her more for me, than she was wont to ask, in her sorrowful and tearful groanings. For Thou didst so convert me to Thyself, that I sought neither wife, nor any hope of this world, standing in that rule of faith, where Thou hadst in a vision revealed me to her so many years before. And Thou didst "turn her mourning into joy" (Ps. 30:11), fuller by far than she had desired ...' Monica had prayed for over thirty years and she was spared nearly two more years to enjoy the answer to her prayers before being taken home to glory to hear her Lord's 'Well done.'

Following conversion in August 386, Augustine gave up his professorship and he and some of his Christian friends devoted themselves to a celibate life of study. In the spring of the following year he was baptised by Ambrose to whom he owed so much. Thereafter he took up the cause of trying to undo what he had done as a Manichee by writing more than a dozen books showing the errors of their teaching. In 388 he left Italy and returned home to Africa, taking care on his travels to avoid towns he knew had no bishop in case he should be pressed into office! That did happen eventually despite his best efforts to avoid it, and he was ordained Bishop of Hippo in North Africa in 396, an office he graced for the following twenty-four years. Monica did not live to see her son a bishop but she did not need to as it was much more important to her to see him born again.

Countering Heresy

God raised Augustine to be a bishop just when and where his mental acuity was most needed. Two great errors were beginning to cause cracks in the Christian church and these required to be countered. Donatism was the first to raise its schismatic head, causing havoc in the African church. Donatists (named after Donatus, Bishop of Casae Nigrae and the theologian Donatus the Great) objected to the election of the bishop of Carthage because they thought that Felix, the bishop who was to consecrate him, was a traitor. The heresies behind their thinking were, one, that only those whose lives were blameless were true Christians and, two, the validly of the sacraments depended on the worthiness of the celebrant. Donatists also rebaptised Christians who came from the Catholic Church into their sect. Augustine countered their arguments and developed the doctrine of the 'invisible church'. He taught that only God knows those who are his own and men cannot distinguish the true believer from the false. The visible church, he said, was just an outward organisation. The invisible church was the true church of God.

Donatism was no sooner losing its following when another sect sprang up to take its place. This time the problem was Pelagianism, called after Pelagius, a British-born monk who had studied law, rhetoric and theology. Pelagius rejected the doctrine of original sin, teaching that man has an inate capacity to seek God and to turn away from evil. According to his thinking, children were born sinless. Not only that, he taught that heaven could be gained either through the law or through grace, and he defined grace as the natural ability given by God that allowed people to seek and serve him. Before the coming of Christ, men could enter heaven by living a moral life, he argued, and that continued to be the case in the Christian era. Countering Pelagianism led Augustine to formulate a biblical theology on the subject. He concluded that we all inherit Adam's sinful nature, even newborn infants, and that we are born with a bias towards sin and an inability to live a righteous life in the eyes of God. Fallen man, he taught, sins both inevitably and according to his own free will. On the subject of those who will one day be in heaven Augustine contended that they are the elect, those whom God has chosen out of all mankind who will ever live, and that not all are chosen. Regarding grace, Augustine said that grace does not find men willing to do

God's will, it makes them willing to do it. God's grace operates before conversion in election and calling, and after conversion in sustaining to the end. In the centuries that have elapsed since then, Donatism and Pelagianism have been at the root of most heresies, and Augustine's thinking has helped the church to counter these false teachings over and over again.

In 410, while the heretical soup was on the boil, Rome fell to barbarian invaders. This raised an interesting theological argument for there were those who claimed that Rome fell because the Roman gods were angry at the spread of Christianity. Augustine's response to this was to write his great apologetic work, The City of God. In it he argued that pagan gods could provide neither health, wealth nor happiness on earth nor in heaven. Christianity, on the other hand, came with the assurance of a heavenly city that would be the eternal home of all who believe through Christ, although it gave no assurance whatever of success or advancement in this world.

Twenty years later, just as a heathen army was planning to rout Hippo, Augustine died. He had been God's man in a turbulent time, and his thinking led the church through many such times in the future. For over 1500, years countless Christians have looked back to the teaching of

Augustine to help clarify their thinking, and over these same years many Christian mothers have looked back to the prayerful Monica for encouragement to keep praying for their wayward children.

Much of Augustine's life before his conversion was so awful that even Monica would have had difficulty imagining how God could possibly use it in her son's ministry. But he did. Augustine's background gave him an understanding of both Christian and Roman culture as he was the product of a mixed marriage. His training in rhetoric sharpened his mental processes and enabled him to present a case more cleverly than the best advocate in a modern courtroom. After his years of study and teaching, Augustine was a very well-known intellectual from Thagaste in North Africa to Milan in the north of Italy, and further still by repute. He was so well-known that when he returned to North Africa after his conversion he had to avoid travelling though any town that did not have a bishop to avoid being appointed!

When he parted company with the Manichees, Augustine studied their teaching so thoroughly that he wrote 'more than two dozen' books to prove them wrong. As a result when Donatism threatened the church he was God's man to oppose it. Firstly, he was African and Donatism began in the African church. Secondly, he had honed his skills when disproving the heretical teachings of the Manichees. Thirdly, his training in rhetoric enabled him to formulate the church's answer to Donatism in as clear a way as possible. Later, when the more serious Pelagianism raised its heretical head, Augustine, with his experience with Donatism, was the obvious person to deal with the new problem that threatened to split the church. Even Augustine's reputation for chaotic living must have been used by the Lord because the purity and chastity of his life after conversion was such a dramatic change, and so consistently lived, that it spoke volumes of the change that the Holy Spirit makes in the lives of God's children.

3

John Bunyan

No book except the Bible has sold as many copies over the years as John Bunyan's Pilgrim's Progress. It has been through many editions and several adaptations since it was written in the second half of the 17th Century. The book has been re-written for children, made into films, even produced as a book to be coloured in by boys and girls too young to read. It has its place as a timeless literary classic, but it is more than that. Pilgrim's Progress captures the interest of adults and children alike because it must surely be the most imaginative account of the Christian life that has ever been written. With roaring lions and giants, raging torrents and sucking mud, the book's potential to captivate its readers is immense, all the more so as they recognise themselves in the story, either as the central character making his painful way to the promised land, or as one of the lesser characters intent on helping or hindering him. But what do we know of the man behind the book? What means did

God use to draw John Bunyan to faith, and is Pilgrim's Progress in fact his testimony?

Little is known of John as a child, but we can be sure that he was an imaginative lad. Pilgrim's Progress was borne out of a fertile imagination well honed through years of use. It is easy to imagine him the centre of a small group of boys, and the one to whom they looked for inspiration for the day's game. No doubt they stalked imaginary giants and fought monsters of all sorts in the woods and byways around Elstow in Bedfordshire, Bunyan's birthplace. And they would have waited for the London to Bedford horse-drawn stagecoach stopping at The Jetty in Elstow's main street to hear the latest news of highwaymen. Elstow was a small village but it was the centre of John Bunyan's world, and it is there we must go to discover his childhood.

John was born to Thomas and Margaret Bunyan in 1628, the year after their marriage. It was a second marriage for Thomas, whose first wife died childless in early 1627. Margaret was born two years later and William in 1633. They lived at Harrowden, just south east of Elstow village, and the family connection there went back over many generations. In fact, there is a record of one William Bunyun in Harrowden as early as 1199. Thomas Bunyan was a tinker by trade, spending his life travelling from village to village repairing pots and pans. It was an occupation that kept his family housed and fed but little more. Perhaps it was his lowly status in society and the poverty of his profession that inspired Thomas to send his oldest child to school. Which school John attended remains a mystery, but it was probably either the village school in Houghton Conquest, three miles from Harrowden, or Harpur Grammar School in Bedford. Although the boy learned to read and write he later admitted that he soon forgot all he had been taught.

A Young Tearaway

Before he was ten years old John had begun to get a name for himself in the area as something of a tearaway, and the years that followed did not improve him. 'Even from a very young age, few could equal me for cursing, swearing, lying and blaspheming the holy name of God. In fact, I grew so accustomed to these things that they became second nature to me.' It was not that John Bunyan knew no better, week by week he was under the sound of preaching that he chose to ignore and defy. However, it seems that the Holy Spirit was moving in his rebellious soul for he recorded that he was troubled with thoughts and nightmares of judgement and hell. His young mind could clearly see demons and evil spirits bound with chains until the Day of Judgement, and the thought that he would be among them tormented his young heart. Perhaps it was to rid his mind of such thoughts that he threw himself into sports and numerous friendships. Unfortunately he chose companions with like interests to his own, and not geared to encourage him to change his ways.

The more thoughts of judgement troubled him the more John involved himself in things that would take his mind off the matter. Having said that, the possibility of reformation must have presented itself to John, as he wrote later, 'I would be deeply cast down in spirit and afflicted in mind. But I could not let go of my sins. I was also so overcome with despair of life and heaven that I often wished either that there were no hell, or that I had been a demon – so that if I had to go there, I would rather be one who tormented others than be tormented myself.' It is necessary – though difficult – to bear in mind that this description is of a nine or ten year old. It displays a spiritual sensitivity that might have led to an early conversion. However, in the case of John Bunyan, it produced a hardness of heart that allowed him to put thoughts of a lost eternity out of his mind in order that he could enjoy life here on earth to the full. So completely did he rid himself of these troubling thoughts that he said it was as though they had never been there in the first place.

As John moved from childhood into his teenage years he gathered about himself a group of companions, and he was their undoubted leader. Sinful and ungodly behaviour was what they enjoyed together. They were not the kind of youths in whom their parents would have taken pride. We will never know the effort it took to keep thoughts of judgement out of his mind, but we do know that when John met real religion it disturbed him, and when he met hypocrisy it disconcerted him badly. The sight of anyone reading pious books was intolerable and upsetting to him, making him feel imprisoned. His choice of 'imprisoned' to describe his reaction would seem to show that his earlier dreams and fears, though out of his conscious mind, were not buried very deeply in his subconscious. Interestingly he had, perhaps, an even stronger reaction to hypocrisy. Christians behaving unchristianly really upset him, and once when he heard a believer swear, it made his heart ache. One wonders if anyone in Elstow recognised the spiritual sensitivity that lurked not far underneath the surface of this youth who was running away from God, or if everyone took him at face value and avoided him.

Cromwell's Army

But for God's providence John might not have grown to manhood. We have three accounts of accidents that might have taken his life, twice by drowning and once when an act of utter stupidity put him in danger. The details of that occasion probably describe better than anything else the type of person that Bunyan had become. 'I struck it (an adder) over the back with a stick I had in my hand and, having stunned it, I forced open its mouth with the stick and plucked its sting out with my fingers…' The John Bunyan we meet in the early 1640s was a young fool, and an anti-social one at that.

In 1644 influenza swept through Bedfordshire and claimed his mother as a victim. Hardly had John become used to the idea of being motherless when his young sister also died. Thomas married again almost immediately. It is hard to imagine the effect of the first three months of that year on the sixteen-year-old, who was by then a tinker like his father. Within weeks of his family trauma John turned his back on his home and signed up as a soldier in Oliver Cromwell's Parliamentary army. The Civil War raged and he set out to fight the King's men. Cromwell's troops were Puritan, but there was one soldier who certainly did not subscribe to their Puritan principles, and he was

John Bunyan. His soldiering years present as much of a mystery as his education, but one fact comes from his own pen, a fact that shows once again God's providential care over a very wayward young man. 'I was chosen along with some others to go to a particular place to lay siege to it. Just as I was about to leave, one of the others asked to take my place. To this request I gave my consent. Coming to the siege, as he stood guard, he was shot in the head by a musket-ball and died.' Even this did not send Bunyan to God in thanksgiving and looking for mercy. Instead, he continued to sin and grew more and more rebellious against God and careless about his own salvation.

It seems that John's military life lasted about three years because we find him back in Elstow in 1647, not improved by his time away or the Puritan influence of Cromwell's men. Within two years he was married. His wife's name is not known; though some assume she was Mary as that was what they called their first child, a little blind girl. Whatever her name, she was the daughter of a godly man, and she brought into her poor marriage home two books: The Plain Man's Pathway to Heaven by Arthur Dent – all 423 pages of it, and The Practise of Piety by Dr Lewis Bayley. Like John his wife had learned to read, but unlike him she remembered what she had been taught. She must have been a woman of some force of character because we know that she often read from these books to her young husband. Not only that, but soon after their marriage she had him attending church every Sunday. John wrote that his wife held up her father to him as an example. 'She would often tell me what a godly man her father was, how he used to reprove and correct sinful behaviour, both in his own home and among his neighbours, and what a strict and holy life he lived in this world, and how this was evident both in his words and deeds.'

What a different home young Mrs Bunyan now lived in compared to the one in which she had been brought up. But she must have been encouraged at the effect her books had on her husband. Hearing them read seems to have given John a desire for a better life than the one he was leading. So much was this the case that he began to seek out the company of people who were known to be religious. Soon he was singing as loud as they were and quoting the Bible too. But his heart, though moved to some reformation of life, was not in the least touched by the spirit of true repentance. In fact, Bunyan claims that this period was marked more by godless superstition than a godly seeking after righteousness. Rather than worshipping God he worshipped the church and all concerned with it. Each part of each service was reverenced, and he put everyone engaged in the Lord's work on a quite unchristian pedestal. All about them filled him with a sense of holiness: their clothes, their bearing, the work they did. Even if he knew a clergyman was leading an ungodly life his feelings about him were just the same.

Not a Jew

Having tempted John Bunyan to worship religion rather than the Lord, Satan went on to tempt him with religious puzzles that could never lead to salvation. He became particularly engrossed in discovering whether he was in any way descended from God's chosen people, the Jews. Had he found that to be the case, John believed he would have found contentment. It is interesting to note that what he was looking for was contentment, peace of mind and heart, rather than salvation from sin. Not knowing where else to discover the answer to his question, he discussed the matter with his father. His hopes were shattered when he was told that there was no Jewish blood in his veins. It is a sad fact that this young man was more interested in finding Jewish blood in his own veins than discovering that the blood of God's Son, himself a Jew, had been shed for the remission of his sins. The truth is, and we have it from Bunyan's own pen, that he never thought of Christ, not even asking himself whether Jesus had existed or did exist. It is not surprising that for all his interest in religion his lifestyle was no better than it had been before.

It was to an aspect of his lifestyle that God spoke to Bunyan through a sermon he heard in church. His minister preached on the fourth commandment, on keeping the Sabbath Day holy. Although John was by then attending church twice most Sundays, the rest of the day was full of other activities. As far as he was concerned Sunday was when he was free from work as a tinker and able to join his friends in all kinds of sporting and leisure activities. This sermon marked a new stage in Bunyan's religious experience. As a child he had often been terrified of God's judgement but that did not lead him to any kind of conviction that he would be judged for his own sins. He seems to have been terrified of judgement in general rather than his own judgement in particular. However, as John listened to his minister on the subject of the Lord's Day he 'felt for the first time what guilt was. … (he) was so laden down with it then that when the sermon had ended, (he) went home heavily burdened in spirit.'

The effect of the sermon was, however, extremely short-lived. Having anguished over the issue until his dinner was cooked, he ate and his conviction passed as quickly as his hunger pangs. After eating his fill he left his wife in their home, put the effect of the sermon from his mind, and went to meet his friends for their usual afternoon of fun together. But God is not so easily dismissed. Right in the middle of their game it was as though a voice spoke from heaven asking, 'Will you leave your sins and go to heaven, or keep your sins and go to hell?' His friends must have wondered what was happening. Bunyan dropped his bat on the ground and looked heavenwards, from where the voice seemed to have come. Suddenly everything clarified in his mind. The Lord was angry with him and threatening him with the dire consequences of his behaviour. No sooner did God reveal to John his sinfulness than the devil insinuated the lie that he had gone too far, that he could not be forgiven. Convinced that he was too great a sinner to be forgiven the young man picked up the bat again and played with a ferocity geared only to take the matter right out of his mind.

On his way home Bunyan considered what had happened. He knew he was a sinner, of that there was no doubt, but he was a hopeless sinner. That being the case, he decided, he was damned whatever he did so he would do everything he could to enjoy himself this side of eternity. That marked the beginning of a time of desperation, where he played his sports with a new drive to win, and where he sought out every sin he could think of intending enjoying them to the full. 'All hope of heaven was already gone,' he wrote later, 'so I could not allow myself to think on that. However, I did find within me a great desire to take my fill of sin, so I continued to consider what sin I could still commit in order that I might taste its sweetness. I made great haste to indulge myself in its delicacies, lest I should die before fulfilling my desires – something that I greatly feared.' For a month he sinned with a will and one can only begin to imagine what his poor young wife, having been brought up in a godly home, made of that.

It was another poor woman who was led to intervene in Bunyan's downward spiral, and from his account she was a 'loose and ungodly woman' herself. As he approached her home he was behaving disgustingly. He was 'playing the madman as usual.' What a row she gave him! In no uncertain terms she told the young man that his speech and behaviour were the worst she had ever heard and seen, that he was a contaminating influence on any who came near him, to the point that he could ruin every young person in town! Having found her tongue, this woman used it to full effect. By the end of her tirade, John Bunyan was standing with his head bowed in shame in front of her. But much more important, his heart was bowed in shame before the Lord. Part of him wished he was a boy again, a boy who had never learned to swear. And part of him still believed that any effort at reformation was condemned before it was undertaken as he was damned in the eyes of God.

Earning a Way to Heaven

A surprise awaited the young man. Before very long had passed he realised he had stopped swearing. John Bunyan, who had sworn from boyhood, and who never seemed to have learned to express himself without an oath, spoke with a new purity of speech! Around the same time, he met with a Christian man and they struck up a friendship. His new friend's interest in the faith led Bunyan to read the Bible and together they discussed God's Word at length. Old Testament history caught his interest and he read it avidly. It is interesting to note that although he had forgotten how to read or write – or at least he had lost them through misuse – he was able to apply himself to reading when he really wanted to do so. The Ten Commandments became the rules of his life and he made strenuous efforts to keep them. His wife must have been delighted at the change, and at his sorrow when he broke God's law. But perhaps she realised that her husband was still unsaved and continued to pray for him. For while John strove for reformation of life he neither understood his need for salvation nor studied the New Testament sufficiently to discover the truth. A year passed with Bunyan trying to earn his way to heaven. Testimony to his efforts is his comment, 'I thought I pleased God as well as any man in England.'

The change in John Bunyan must have been the talk of the town. Having been notorious for his swearing and godless behaviour, he now became known for his apparent piety. His conversation was peppered with Bible verses, his life was unimpeachable, and his home became a quiet and happy haven. It is little wonder that the neighbours talked about it. Some even commented to John himself about the changes in his life; and he liked what he heard. Nothing seems to have pleased him better than hearing how good he was. That being the case we can be sure that although he was reformed in terms of his behaviour he was certainly not converted. There was not a shred of humility in John Bunyan. The word hypocrite springs to mind, but that suggests deliberate play-acting. The events that follow show that he was living in heathen ignorance rather than being hypocritical.

One of Bunyan's hobbies was bell-ringing. He enjoyed it hugely, but God seemed to show him that bell-ringing was a form of vanity. It is not clear whether that meant it engendered vanity in him as a person, or whether he believed that the practice was a vain one. However, having given up ringing, John could not quite break away and he took to standing around listening to the other bell-ringers as they practised. That was when a terrible thought invaded his mind. What would happen if one of the bells were to fall? Such a terror took hold of him that John sought the safety of the steeple door. Then he suddenly thought that the steeple door might collapse. That kept him away from the bell-ringers! Dancing was another thing he gave up. A comment he made describing this stage of his experiences is a dire warning to religious people who are unconverted. 'When I thought I kept one or another of the commandments, or did by word or deed anything I thought was good, I had great peace in my conscience and would think to myself, "God cannot but be pleased with me now."' Only later did he realise, 'Poor sinner that I was, I was all this time ignorant of Jesus Christ and trying to establish my own righteousness. I would have perished in it had God, in mercy, not revealed to me more of my natural state.'

Godly Women

Bunyan's work as a tinker meant that he travelled the area around Elstow mending pots, pans and other tinware. His work often took him to

Bedford, and it was when he was there one day that he came across a little group of women sitting at a door talking about the Lord. Now well able to take part in religious discussions, John approached the women with a view to joining in their conversation. But what he heard both disquieted and quietened him. This was no theoretical discussion of theology or mulling over the finer points of some verse or other. These women were using words with which he was unfamiliar. They were not so much discussing religion as sharing their own Christian experiences, something totally new to John Bunyan. It says much of the working of God in his heart that he listened to what these women said rather than joining in and trying to impress them with his cleverness.

What was it that so affected him? For the first time it seems that his heart was soft enough to recognise true Christian piety. These women had obviously had personal experiences of the Lord for their conversation covered conviction of sin, spiritual rebirth, the work of Satan, God's promises and his faithfulness in keeping them. John listened enthralled. Hearing the words caused an ache in his heart even through he didn't understand what they were speaking about. These pious women talked about their good deeds being as filthy rags in God's sight while he felt that God must be mightily pleased with him. Yet for all the women mourned over their shortcomings there was a joy in them that Bunyan knew he did not possess. 'They spake as if joy did make them speak; they spake with such pleasantness of Scripture language, and with such appearance of grace in all they said, that they were to me as if they had found a new world.' Although John did not know it, these women were among the twelve members of the Puritan Free Church that had recently opened in Bedford under the ministry of John Gifford.

The effect that little group of women had on John Bunyan was such that he looked for excuses to work in their area of Bedford just in order to hear more of their conversation. A deep longing grew within him as he listened to their talk. Bunyan was surprised by two things, and they did surprise him as he knew that he was an 'ungodly wretch': one was the great tenderness of heart he felt in the company of the faithful women, and the other was how much what they said stayed in his mind. When he was with them his thoughts, he said, were so fixed on the things of eternity that he didn't want to let go of them. 'It would then have been as difficult for me to have dragged my thoughts back from heaven to earth as I have often found it since to shift them from earth to heaven.' Reading the Bible became 'sweet and pleasant' although what he read sometimes sent Bunyan into a torment of doubt. Temptation also came from the direction of some of his 'religious' friends, a number of whom had become Ranters, members of a sect that engaged in all kinds of 'vile behaviour'. But although temptations such as they presented appealed to his sinful nature, he had begun to see the light of better things.

There were battles still to be fought on the road to faith and one of them must have made his wife wonder, if she knew anything about it. John Bunyan decided that the only way he could be sure if he had faith was if he could perform a miracle. Scripture verses taken out of context reinforced him in this error. As he travelled one showery day between Elstow and Bedford he decided on the perfect miracle to test his faith. He would tell puddles to be dry and dry places to become puddles. However, just as he was about to speak it was borne in on him that he should pray first. Having prayed he returned to his puddles. But an awful thought came into his mind before he ordered them to be dry. If the miracle didn't work despite his having prayed first then all he would prove was that he was eternally lost. Fearful of discovering that to be the case he abandoned the idea and went on his way in great confusion of mind.

Doubts and Fears

The subject of election troubled him greatly in the months after that. Thinking about it drove him to his wit's end, to use his own expression. It was not the doctrine of election that caused Bunyan problems, he seems to have accepted that. What troubled him was that he doubted he was one of the elect. Knowing that only the elect obtain eternal life he despaired of knowing if he was among that number. In the midst of his turmoil it was as though he was told to begin at the beginning of Genesis and read through to the end of Revelation to see if anyone who ever trusted God was cast away, or if all true followers stayed the course to the end. The words, 'Look at the generations of old and see, did any of them trust in God, and be cast away?' were given to him at the same time. Bunyan read through the Bible to find out if this was true and to find the words that had come into his mind. For more than a year he searched the Scriptures before he eventually found the verse in the Apocryphal book of Ecclesiasticus. By the time he found it, his reading of the whole of God's Word had to a degree settled his mind on the subject.

After a time, however, his thoughts were assaulted by the possibility that although nobody was ever turned away who came to the Lord in faith, it might be that the day of grace was over, that he had had his opportunity to believe and had not grasped it when it was held out to him. It took God speaking powerfully to Bunyan from Luke 14 to quell that fear. 'Compel them to come in, that my house may be filled … and still there is room.' How comforting the words 'and still there is room' were to his troubled heart. But the comfort only lasted for a time and before long he was again in the Slough of Despond about which, years later, he was to write so powerfully in Pilgrim's Progress. 'I began to sink greatly into despair and I began to entertain such discouragement in my heart that I was laid low as hell. Had I burned at the stake now, I could not believe that Christ loved me.' It is little wonder that his writing was so vivid, because he was describing his own experience.

Although John Bunyan was under great conviction of sin, those who knew him saw a change in his life and watched and waited to see if it would pass. His new friends in Bedford were less cynical, and realising that he was truly seeking a Saviour they told John Gifford, their minister, about him. It must have been a surprise to the twenty-five year-old tinker to learn that the Puritan minister, whom he so much admired, had been reckless, a gambler, drinker and a blasphemer as well. At last Bunyan had found someone who understood what he was going through and who would walk with him on his journey to faith. Gifford not only had a private past, he also had a public past as there had been a time when he had persecuted the Puritans in Bedford. He must have been a big man to remain in the same town after he was converted, with a big enough heart to be patient with John Bunyan. From their first meeting, at which the young tinker poured out his problems, the two men became firm friends.

At the Cross

John often visited Gifford to discuss what was in his heart and on his mind. Not only that, he enjoyed listening to the minister talking with others about their souls and learned from what he heard. The nearer John came to faith the more conscious he was of his sins. Then the day came when, after years of struggle, Bunyan saw the light of the truth that righteousness is only to be found in the Person of Christ and in him alone. The journey to faith had been tortuous but the man who sought found, and was soundly converted. Although there were fears and doubts still to be faced there was no doubt about Bunyan's conversion. John Gifford, fine Puritan that he was, would not have accepted into membership anyone who was unable to give a good account of God's saving grace. When Bunyan wrote Pilgrim's Progress, Pilgrim lost his burden at the cross and John lost his there too.

Pilgrim still had a difficult journey to travel before he entered the Celestial City and so did John.

Having been greatly helped by Gifford's preaching and counsel, John moved his wife and children into Bedford to be under his ministry. More people attended the little Puritan church as they were impressed by the change in the tinker they had known well in his rebellious years. John Gifford's ministry was not to last much longer, however, as he died in 1655. The church was without a minister for several months. Then John Burton, a man of like mind, was appointed to the charge. It was about this time that Bunyan began preaching, perhaps by helping fill the pulpit during the vacancy. Within a short time he had a travelling ministry, preaching in homes, farm buildings, and in the open-air where there was no alternative or too large a crowd. Having travelled the area as a tinker Bunyan was well-known, and his sinful excesses were clearly remembered. People who came out of interest to hear what had happened to him often found themselves captivated by God's power through his preaching. He was not without his enemies who both doubted his right to preach and criticised his style. But believing God had called him to preach, and that the Puritan Church in Bedford had endorsed his call, Bunyan was not put off by his detractors.

In 1658 the Bunyans had a fourth child, but his wife did nor recover from her confinement and died soon afterwards. A widower at thirty, with young children, one of them blind, John faced a real test of faith. After struggling with his family for over a year he remarried, and this time we know his wife's name. She was Elizabeth, and she was a source of real strength to him. About the time of his marriage John Burton died and once again the faithful little congregation was left without a minister. They were also left without a building in which to worship as the church was reclaimed by the Established Church. Not only were there changes in Bedford, there was upheaval throughout England because Oliver Cromwell, the great champion of the Puritan cause, was dead and the country was once again a monarchy. Charles II, having promised 'liberty to tender consciences' lulled non-conformists into thinking that they were safe to continue their preaching ministries, John Bunyan among them. But it was not to be. Before long, use of the Book of Common Prayer was being enforced by magistrates throughout the country, including in the town of Bedford. Bunyan, and those who shared his evangelical beliefs, viewed the Book of Common Prayer with grave suspicion. At best they thought it was too high church, and at worse they condemned it as Roman Catholic.

Come, Be of Good Cheer

Refusal to use the Book of Common Prayer could mean imprisonment, and Bunyan knew that when he went to preach in Lower Samsell, a hamlet twelve miles from Bedford, in November 1660. On arrival there he discovered that a warrant had been issued for his arrest. When his host suggested cancelling the service, Bunyan's reply was firm. 'No, no! by no means. I will not stir, neither will I have the meeting dismissed for this. Come, be of good cheer; let us not be daunted. Our cause is good, we need not be ashamed of it; to preach God's Word is so good a work that we shall be well rewarded… even if we suffer for it.' Bunyan led the congregation in prayer and announced his text, 'Dost thou believe on the Son of God?' (John 9:35 KJV) before being interrupted by the constable thrusting the warrant for his arrest into the preacher's hand. He was ordered to appear before the Justice the following morning. 'Brethren and sisters,' said Bunyan, looking over the distracted congregation, 'we are prevented of our opportunity to speak and hear the Word of God, and we are like to suffer for this attempt to do so … It is a mercy to suffer upon so good account. For might we not have been apprehended as thieves and murderers, or for other wickedness? …But, blessed be God, it is not so! We suffer as Christians for well-doing…'

The following morning Bunyan was committed to the jail in Bedford to await a hearing. 'I held my peace,' he said, 'and, blessed be the Lord, went away to prison, with God's comfort in my poor soul.' Not only did Elizabeth have to bear the burden of having her husband imprisoned just five minutes walk along the road from her home, but she went into premature labour and lost their child.

Nearly two months later John stood to hear the indictment. 'That John Bunyan, of the town of Bedford, labourer, being a person of such and such conditions, hath devilishly and perniciously abstained from coming to church to hear Divine service, and is a common upholder of several unlawful meetings and conventicles, to the great disturbance and distraction of the good subjects of this kingdom, contrary to the laws of our sovereign lord the King...' To the charge that he abstained from coming to church, John answered. 'I am a frequenter of the Church of God, and by grace a member with those people over whom Christ is the Head.' When accused of not using the Book of Common Prayer, he told his accusers, 'We pray with the Spirit, and with the understanding.' The trial – which must have sounded more like a General Synod met to discuss the Book of Common Prayer – eventually drew to its conclusion, a foregone conclusion. Bunyan was sentenced to three months in Bedford prison, and if at the end of that time his mind had not changed he was in danger of being banished from England. It must have taken the Justice aback when, instead of crumbling at the thought of punishment, Bunyan stood his full height and said, 'Sir, as to this matter, I am at a point with you; for if I am out of prison today, I will preach the gospel again tomorrow – by the help of God.'

It seems that John Bunyan found favour with some of the prison guards as he was sometimes allowed out. His congregation's records show that he attended occasional meetings. It is even known that he took services from time to time in farm buildings and in the open-air. In his cell he had his Bible and a copy of Foxe's Book of Martyrs, and when he was not studying he made leather laces to sell for the support of his family. It was when John was in prison that he discovered the kind of woman he had married, and to whom he had entrusted the care of his children. He and Elizabeth wrote a petition asking for his pardon. Showing great courage, Elizabeth took a copy all the way to the House of Lords in London. As there is nothing to suggest that she was not from as humble a background as her husband this was not only an act of great courage but one of mind-blowing audacity! She presented the petition to Lord Barkwood who, after discussion with others of the Upper House, told Elizabeth that her husband could only be released at a local hearing. That was not the end of her efforts. When the Midsummer Assize was due she intercepted both judges to gave them copies of the petition. And when it seemed that all else had failed she gate-crashed a meeting of the judges and the local gentry to present Bunyan's case. Finally they lost patience and demanded to know if her husband would give up preaching if he were released. 'My Lord, he dares not leave preaching as long as he can speak.' That short sentence shows courage, dignity and faith. It was only when she was told that the judges could do nothing, and that she should seek a pardon from the king, that the good woman broke down and wept.

While Elizabeth was fighting for his freedom, Bunyan was using his time in prison wisely. And he had plenty of time, for prison was where he spent all but a short period of the next twelve years. Having previously written some tracts – this was the man who once forgot how to read and write – he spent many hours writing and A Discourse Touching Prayer was published from his prison cell. Grace Abounding to the Chief of Sinners appeared four years later in 1666. It was an account of his life and how God dealt with his soul. Had they but known it, the authorities that put Bunyan in prison and held him there assured a wide circulation for his books. He had gained a certain fame, not to say notoriety, that encouraged people to read them.

Pilgrim's Progress

For the four years between 1672 and 1676 the religious and political climate changed and Bunyan was released. Those were profitable years spent ministering to the congregation in Bedford until he was again imprisoned for a time. While his circumstances changed Bunyan was constant in his writing, and his greatest book was still to come. It was almost as though he was honing his literary skills before spending five years writing Pilgrim's Progress which was first published in 1678. The book was an instant best-seller. Remarkably it sold 100,000 copies in its first ten years. The Life and Death of Mr Badman followed, then The Holy War. But it is for Pilgrim's Progress that John Bunyan is remembered.

Is Pilgrim's Progress John Bunyan's testimony? It is an allegory of the Christian life and certainly contains many of the experiences he went through. Evangelist was to Pilgrim what John Gifford was to Bunyan. Both his wives could have modelled Faithful in the book. And in Grace Abounding to the Chief of Sinners he takes us through the Slough of Despond and the Valley of the Shadow, as well as Vanity Fair and Doubting Castle. Giant Despair is also straight from his own experiences. Whether or not Pilgrim follows in rigid detail the spiritual journey that Bunyan undertook is of interest rather than important as the message of the book stands whichever is the case. What is sure is that when John Bunyan died in 1688 there was a welcome for him in the Celestial City, just as there was for Pilgrim.

John Bunyan is a magnificent example of someone whose unregenerate past was, in the providence of God, his gift to the future. When he was in the depths of despair he could not have known that Giant Despair would grow out of that trial and help millions – and it is millions – of people going through the same thing. Nor could he ever have guessed that when the poor but pious women introduced him to the good John Gifford they introduced him to Evangel, the man who would point him to Christ. Of course, Bunyan's Christian life is also told in essence in Pilgrim's Progress and that has been an equal encouragement to its readers over the last three and a quarter centuries. But not only were Bunyan's 'lost' years redeemed in literature, they were a blessing to those to whom he preached during his lifetime.

Because he was known for his dissolute lifestyle people flocked to hear him when they heard that he had been converted, no doubt many of them interested to see just how long the change would last before he would be back out on the sports field on a Sunday and swearing when his team lost. And of course that notoriety made those who had heard of him want to read his books. God, in his providence, took John's 'sins and faults of youth' and used them as tools in the building of his kingdom.

4

Selina, The Countess of Huntingdon

Astwell Manor House near Brackley in Northamptonshire was the birthplace of Selina Shirley in August 1707. If ever a child was born into a sad and dysfunctional family, Selina was. And it was not just of her parents' making. Troubles had followed the Shirley family for generations. Her great-grandfather, Sir Robert, died in the Tower of London and his death was 'not without suspicion of poison.' He had spent years in the Tower for being a follower of the banished royal house of Stuart. His son, a second Robert, was born shortly before his father's imprisonment and was therefore brought up in a fatherless household, if a privileged one. In 1671, when he was only twenty years of age he married Elizabeth Washington who was five years his junior and before long the first of his large family was born.

Whether nor not the first Sir Robert was guilty of complicity with the Stuarts is a moot point, but his son had a mind of his own in religious matters. After the Restoration in 1660 young Sir Robert made known his allegiance to Charles II, and six years later he reaped his reward in the baronetcy of Ferrers. But Charles II was soon to be succeeded by his brother James, a Roman Catholic. Unwilling to support a Catholic crown, Sir Robert sought another cause to follow, and found it in the daughter of James II, the Protestant Princess Anne. That was a politically astute move. When she ascended the throne in 1702 Anne found a loyal supporter in Sir Robert, and she needed all the support she could get.

Children were born to the Shirleys in quick succession, at least eleven in twenty two years of marriage, of which nine survived childhood. This speaks of a healthy pedigree, and there were few better pedigrees in England than the combination of the Shirleys and the Washingtons. The Shirleys could trace their ancestry back to Saxon times, and the Washingtons could likewise look back with pride on their aristocratic past. What they did not then know was that they could also look forward to one George Washington who was to become the first President of the United States. Elizabeth Washington Shirley died young. Aged just thirty seven, and worn out by her many confinements, she bore her last son in 1693 and died soon afterwards.

Nine motherless children, aged from twenty years down to an infant, must have made for a sad home. But more sadness was to come. In the six years that followed Elizabeth's death, Sir Robert seems to have quarrelled with every one of his children, at least with those of an age to disagree with him seriously. In 1699 he married for a second time, and a year later the first child of six who survived childhood from that marriage was born. Was it currying favour, or was it a mark of friendship, when he asked Queen Anne to be godmother to his youngest child? Whichever it was, it was followed just months later with the title First Earl of Ferrers and Viscount Tamworth. Sir Robert Shirley was well in with the royal circle of his day and he seems to have been a particular favourite of the queen.

While things might have been happy between Sir Robert and the throne, they were decidedly less happy in his home. Relations with the children of his first marriage were poor at best. Nothing bears testimony to that more than the fact that when he died, the First Earl of Ferrers virtually disinherited his children by his first marriage in favour of those born to his second wife. So it was that his second son, Washington Shirley (whose older brother was by then dead), who might reasonably have expected to inherit the bulk of the family's vast fortune in land, found himself fobbed off with the grand title of Second Earl of Ferrers and very little of material value. Consequently, the death of Sir Robert formalised a breakdown in family relationships that was to have repercussions down through the years to our subject, Washington's daughter Selina, who became the Countess of Huntingdon. She was ten years old when her father learned how little he had meant to his father. One can only imagine what she heard in her home when it was discovered that her grandfather had left £5000 to several of his children and a derisory £20 to her father for mourning 'and no more'. Even his full brothers received five times that. Selina's teenage years and early adult life was lived against the backdrop of claims and counter claims, appeals and further appeals in the courts of the land. And, as anyone knows who has read books about that period, there were few winners in Chancery apart from the professionals employed there.

Home Life

Selina's family history alone would have caused pressures and tensions in her young life, but that was not all with which she had to contend. To understand Selina we have not only to look back through the years that preceded but deeply affected her, but we must also look within her own home. Washington Shirley married Mary Levinge around the beginning of the 18th Century; no record of the marriage or the births of their three daughters are extant. In fact, it seems that they were not recorded in the Shirley family records, which speaks volumes of the relationship Washington had with his family. Mary was a woman of property who no doubt assumed that she was marrying into the vast wealth of the Shirleys. And as she married Washington after the death of his older brother her expectations would be high. Although the young couple's prospects seemed good, Washington was virtually left to provide for himself and he did that by serving as an officer of humble rank in the Coldstream Guards. He was on a posting to Ireland when his first daughter, Elizabeth was born. The child, who was probably born in 1704, was most likely named after her paternal grandmother.

Two years later, with his wife again pregnant, Washington returned to England. If he came to seek reconciliation with his father his efforts were to no avail, even after he called his second daughter Selina after his stepmother. A third daughter Mary, was born some years later, by which time the family was back in Ireland where they remained for much of Selina's childhood. When we try to imagine the family in which she was brought up, we think of a relatively impoverished immediate family connected to all the right people, from the queen down. Her half aunts, uncles and cousins lived in some luxury and affection with her paternal grandfather, while her full relations were hardly on speaking term with him.

Even as quite a young child Selina was noted for her seriousness. A connection of hers wrote a two-volume biography in which he describes her. 'Lady Selina's mind, even in very early infancy, was of a serious cast. When she was only nine years of age, the sight of a corpse, about her own age, on its way to the grave, induced her to attend the burial. There the first impressions of deep seriousness concerning an eternal world took possession of her heart, and with many tears she earnestly implored God, on the spot, that whenever he should be pleased to take her away, he would deliver her from all her fears, and give her a happy departure. She often afterwards visited that grave, and always preserved a lively sense of the affecting scene she had there witnessed.' He went on to note, one assumes of her teenage years, 'Though no correct views of evangelical truth had hitherto enlightened her Ladyship's mind, yet even during her juvenile days, she frequently retired, for prayer, to a particular closet, where she could not be observed, and in all her little troubles found relief in pouring out the feelings of her heart to God. When she grew up and was introduced into the world, she continued to pray that she might marry into a serious family.' Were there particular 'little troubles' that the young Selina had to bear? There were indeed, as we will shortly see.

Her relation and biographer tells us something of the nature of Selina Shirley. Even allowing for a degree of hagiography she does seem to have been an extraordinary personality. She 'was, unquestionably, formed for eminence. Her tender age exhibited a fine dawn of her mature excellence; and she gave early presages of proving highly useful and ornamental to society, if permitted to arrive at those years necessary for maturing the powers of the human mind. Her endowments were much above the ordinary standard. She possessed a highly intelligent mind, and extraordinary quickness of apprehension, a brilliant fancy, a retentive memory, a strong clear understanding, and a sound judgment, much improved by reading, conversation, deep thought and observation. Her knowledge of mankind, even at an early age, and her penetration into the characters of those with whom she was acquainted, were admirable.'

Selina seems to have had a way of getting to the essence of the people with whom she had to do, and that would have made a fascinating study for her had the most complex of them not been her own parents. When she was just six years old Selina's youngest sister was born, but before many months had passed her mother and infant sister left the family home and never returned. The two Marys thereafter lived between homes in France and Spain. Washington was left to bring up his older daughters. Money was a constant problem for him, and it may be that was a contributory factor leading to the breakdown of the marriage. However, it seems from family letters that although he only had three children by his wife, he had several others by extra-marital relationships. Washington Shirley was the child of a fractured family and he went on to produce a family as fractured as his own. Today we hear much of amicable separations and divorces, but that adjective could never have been applied to the Shirley situation. Although her parents had contact over her teenage years, it seems to have been in the form of battles by letter and court case rather than any effort to work together civilly towards the upbringing of their three children.

Washington Shirley had suffered from a poor relationship with his father, and he seems to have learned from that, for he and Selina were bound together by a strong bond of love and affection. In a day when restraint would have been the norm, he and his 'Linny' were not slow to express themselves.

Having written to her in warm terms, Washington would finish his letters with, 'My dear, your most loving father,' or something else equally tender. When they were apart father and daughter wrote regularly to each other, which brings us to one of Selina's interesting characteristics. Although she and her sister must have had a tutor it may be that financial constraints meant that his qualifications were lower than they might have been, because for all her undoubted intelligence and mental acuity, Selina's writing – particularly her spelling – were poor all her life. It may be that an expert looking at her letters today would suspect that she suffered from dyslexia. While affection marked her correspondence with her father, any letters written to her mother were framed in the most formal and businesslike terms. This is evidenced by Selina addressing her mother as 'Madam'. There seems to have been no warmth left in that relationship. What Selina made of her home situation one can only imagine, especially as it was set against the backdrop of the previous generation of Shirleys. Perhaps it is understandable that she prayed she would marry into a serious family.

A Discerning and Contemplative Mind

Seriousness seems to have been a mark of the young Selina Shirley. According to her relative,

'Though she was obliged, from her situation in life, to mix with others in fashionable amusements, an attachment to them, or to the ornament of dress, was not the foible of her discerning and contemplative mind. ... At a very early period in life (she) discovered an elevated turn of mind: she was impressed with a deep sense of divine things, a feeling which had a powerful influence on her conduct, in leading her to read the word of God with great diligence. She manifested an extraordinary turn for religious meditation; and repeatedly felt the most awful convictions of the certainty and eternal duration of a future state. Her conversation was modest, and her whole conduct marked with a degree of rectitude not usually to be found in early life.' Perhaps it is out of loyalty that he makes no mention of her 'choleric temper', a failing she shared with many of the Shirleys. She had that, at least, in common with her grandfather.

As a young woman Selina prayed for marriage into a serious family, and the family into which the Lord led her was, at first glance, as seriously fractured as her own. The Hastings family was as aristocratic as the Shirleys and had lands in the same part of Leicestershire. As the 9th Earl of Huntington (a Hastings) married twice and produced two families, the potential was there for problems of inheritance. But the Huntingdons were a different breed. Far from suffering from the choleric temper that bedevilled the Shirleys, they seem to have been a singularly laid back set of people. Edwin Welch, in his Spiritual Pilgrim, suggests that 'some of them could be described as lethargic.' To bear this out he quotes the inscription Selina put on the monument on her husband's grave when he died after their happy and peaceful marriage. 'Despairing to do National Good, He mingled as little as his Rank permitted in National affairs.' When she married Theophilus, the 9th Earl of Huntingdon, Selina must have heaved a sigh of relief as she enjoyed the peacefulness of happy family life for the first time. Her past did not, however, escape her. Witness to that is a letter written to Selina by her father regarding correspondence from her mother. 'I must desire if you, and my Lord, think proper that you would lend me my wife's letter ... she wrote me one not long since, but I believe that is not of that stile, for it was of such a sort, that I never can forget, or forgive ...'

Lady Bountiful

The home founded at Donnington Park on the marriage of Theophilus and Selina on 3rd June 1728, was of quite a different order, and the setting in which it flourished was too. Her husband was on the best of terms with his half-siblings, referring to them as 'My dears'. One hesitates to think how Washington might have referred to his. And Theophilus must have been a generous man for Washington was unable provide Selina's dowry at the time of their marriage. Instead, he gave a mortgage on one of his estates to his son-in-law, an estate whose ownership was in the process of being decided in Chancery! The young Countess Huntingdon started out as she meant to continue. 'After her marriage, she manifested a particularly serious deportment; and though sometimes at Court, yet, in visiting the higher circles, she took no pleasure in the fashionable follies of the great,' her relative records. 'At Donnington Park, she was the Lady Bountiful among her neighbours and dependants; though, as she afterwards felt and declared, going about to establish her own righteousness, she endeavoured, by prayer, and fasting, and alms-deeds, to commend herself to the favour of the Most High.' From this we paint a picture of the young Countess of Huntingdon (she married at twenty when Theophilus was thirty two). Serious-minded by nature, impatient of 'fashionable follies', she seems to have set out to collect credits in the eyes of God that she hoped would assure her eternal salvation. Though her efforts would win her no favour with the Almighty, they certainly built her up in the esteem of those around Donnington Park, though even there her quick temper was noted.

Unlike Selina, her husband was widely travelled, having undertaken a grand tour of some considerable length. He spent three years on the continent, much longer than many of his contemporaries. It may be that when he eventually returned to England he was ready to settle down, for it seems that is just what he did. Within a year of their marriage a son and heir was born. Washington Shirley had hoped to attend his baptism, but his health was not up to the journey and he had other things on his mind. 'I am not only in a very ill state of health,' he wrote to Selina, excusing his absence, 'but I have an affair to settle with your mother that prevents me.' Two days later, even before the infant Francis' baptism, Washington was dead. Family disputations surrounded his death no less than they had his life. And Selina, who no doubt longed to show her firstborn son to her much-loved father was never able to do so. Washington's estranged wife's reaction to his death was to file a legal claim against Selina and her sisters. The Countess of Huntingdon was never really able to put her family's past behind her; it dogged almost her entire life.

The Hastings family provided an altogether different experience for the young woman; she even found a mother figure for the first time since she was six years old. Theophilus's half-sister Elizabeth (Betty), who was thirteen years older than him, therefore twenty five years older than Selina, was the mothering sort. She was thoughtful and generous to a fault. Perhaps it was her all-embracing nature that helped cement the two parts of the Hastings family together. Selina appears to have modelled herself on this good woman. Consequently, we find that she supported the same kinds of causes as her sister-in-law and in an equally bountiful way. Within a year of her marriage there is a record of her buying Bibles and Prayer Books for distribution. A month or two later a donation of £10 was sent to the Society for the Propagation of Christian Knowledge, and that was a considerable sum in 1729. She not only supported the SPCK financially, she also bought books from them to give to the people around Donnington Park. The young Countess had a bent in the direction of the Lord even though she was still a stranger to grace.

In the first ten years of their eighteen years of happy married life, the Huntingdon's produced seven children, six of whom survived. Childbearing took its toll of Selina, and after the birth of their fourth child in four years she went to Bath to take the waters, and not for the last time. Her visits to Bath for the good of her health resulted in love letters going between herself and her husband, letters that are still in existence and that show their marriage to be deep and loving. Her poorly written epistles, full of affectionate sentiments to her 'dearest Lordship' about 'their little angels' were answered by his efforts, and they were an effort. His sister, Lady Betty, was taken aback that he could 'overcome his aversion to writing' and do so so often! Having said that, he did sometimes employ his secretary to write letters to his wife.

The serious-minded Selina decided that Bath was 'the most stupid place (she) ever yet saw'. Fortunately a sister-in-law and brother-in-law were already there to help take her mind off the stupidity of it. Bath was where the rich and famous were, and where they spent their money to no good effect other than on entertaining themselves. Selina, having been brought up most frugally, found that an irritation. It may even have triggered off her choleric temper on occasions. Although through her husband she was a wealthy woman she never lost her habit of frugality. It does seem that Selina was in Bath for medical treatment. She was a patient of a Scottish doctor who practised there. Dr George Cheyne recommended the waters and a diet to Selina, these to be supplemented by purgings that must have wracked her poor body terribly. Dr Cheyne does not seem to have been keen on watching his own diet as he was estimated to be the heaviest man in England at somewhere in the region of thirty two stones. Selina continued to visit Bath, sometimes for many weeks at a time, until her family was complete with the birth of Henry in 1739. Dr Cheyne reckoned that only adherence to his treatment regime saved his patient from dying 'miserably of cancer of her bowels'.

Selina, the Businesswoman

The Countess of Huntingdon took her role as an Earl's wife seriously, and was very much part of his business dealings. Even when she was on extended visits to Bath (and presumably, therefore, not in good health) she continued to hold the reins of the Donnington Park household. And when she was at home she was as likely to be chasing up unpaid rents as her husband was. In fact, the natures of the pair of them suggest that anything requiring as much effort as the chasing up of unpaid rents would be left to Selina. Documentary evidence tends to substantiate this. And when other homes were being bought, rented or refurbished she was right there making whatever decisions needed to be made. The Countess had a good business head and the energy to put her decisions into bricks, mortar, and the hiring and firing of staff. To all intents and purposes Selina was perhaps even more than Theophilus hoped for. But what was happening in the soul of our subject?

Selina's relation and biographer wrote that the Countess 'was an absolute stranger to that inward and universal change of heart, wrought by the gracious operations of the Spirit of God, by which new principles are established in the mind, new inclinations are imparted, and new objects pursued.' In other words, the good Countess of Huntingdon was greatly respected by those with whom she came in touch but she was a lost sinner in the eyes of God. Faith Cook, in her book Selina, Countess of Huntingdon, suggests that 'the loss of an infant daughter, their fifth child, also named Selina, shortly after her birth in June 1735 added to her sense of the meaninglessness of her way of life. With her own erratic health, the death of her baby, and being disowned by her mother, it is little wonder she was disconsolate.' While God was preparing Selina's heart for the gospel, he was also training men to preach it. Oxford University was the training ground, and the young men's names were to become famous: John and Charles Wesley, Benjamin Ingham, George Whitefield and Howell Harris. But work needed done in the Countess's heart for had she heard their preaching any earlier than she did, Selina would have discounted their efforts as rantings and ravings. There was already a family connection with the 'Holy Club' as Lady Betty Hastings helped finance Whitefield through university, though for philanthropic rather than spiritual reasons.

It was probably when the Huntingdons were in London at the end of 1738 that they first heard more than the name of George Whitefield as he had just returned from a visit to the United States. Crowds gathered to hear his preaching, though the crowds were more likely to gather outside churches than inside as Whitefield was barred (along with the other members of the Holy Club) from preaching in the Established Church. It is not known whether Theophilus and Selina heard him preach, but as Whitefield was the talk of the town they could not but have heard what he said. His message was uncompromising: salvation is by grace alone and cannot be achieved by good works or respectability. For a woman who had based her life on good works and personal acts of piety that was not comforting.

Thus the family had one tenuous connection with Whitefield and they were soon to have another. Theophilus' old tutor at Oxford, Martin Benson, by then Bishop of Gloucester, wrote to his former student telling him that he was about to ordain George Whitefield. 'Though mistaken on some points I think him a very pious, well-meaning young man, with good abilities and great zeal. … I pray God grant him great success in all his undertakings for the good of mankind and a revival of true religion and holiness in these degenerate days; in which prayer I am sure your lordship and my kind good Lady Huntingdon will most heartily join.' Benson showed himself a shrewd judge of character when he accepted Whitefield for ordination, though his judgment on Selina's reaction was probably a little less accurate.

Noisy Protest

A few months later quite a different side to the Countess's character is seen, and her political views became public. The House of Lords was due to discuss appeasement with Spain, a subject on which she felt very strongly. With a group of like-minded women the Countess decided to attend the debate. However, due to the high feeling the subject generated the Lords agreed to hold the debate in private. Undaunted, the women gathered outside the House of Lords, pushed their way to the closed door of the gallery and protested loudly, knowing very well that they would be heard inside. The Lords continued their debate, thinking that their stamina would outlast that of the protestors, and that seemed to be the case when the women fell silent in the late afternoon. Assuming that the protesters had left the gallery the door was opened from the inside, and the women – who had decided that silence might achieve what noise had not – stormed past the doorman who had no way of stopping them. From then until 11 pm the Countess of Huntingdon and her friends noisily disrupted the debate. Selina may have been the picture of propriety, but when her mind was firm on a subject she was prepared to stand up and be counted. The courage that saw her protesting publicly in the House of Lords was soon to be called into Christian service. The pieces of God's jigsaw were fitting into place.

Not many months later Benjamin Ingham, who had acquired quite a name for himself as a formidable and forthright preacher, was invited to preach in the private chapel of Lady Betty's home in Ossett, Yorkshire. Her half-sisters Margaret, Frances and Anne were affected by his preaching. Margaret was the first to come to saving faith, then Frances and Anne. Being a close family it was not long before Margaret testified to her faith to Selina in letters. It is interesting to try to imagine Selina's thoughts as she read these letters and anticipated a visit to Ossett with her husband. Would she find her sisters-in-law greatly changed? Would there still be deep affection between them? Had Margaret's strange spiritual experience taken away the balance of her mind? As she had heard the reputation of the Holy Club preachers such thoughts must have gone through the Countess's mind and may well have troubled her. Having come from an unhappy family into one where there was love and concord it would have been all the more important to her that things did not interfere with the relationships that were most precious. In the early summer of 1739, when the Huntingdons left home to travel to Ossett to visit the family there, she probably felt deep apprehension as well as glad anticipation at the prospect of a time of family reunion.

Conversing with Lady Margaret one day on spiritual matters, Selina was exceedingly struck with a sentiment she uttered, 'That since she had known and believed in the Lord Jesus Christ, for life and salvation, she had been as happy as an angel,' her relation records. But while Lady Margaret was enjoying her newly-found joy, her sister-in-law certainly was not. The same source describes her spiritual state. 'A dangerous illness having, soon after, brought her to the brink of the grave, the fear of death fell terribly upon her, and her conscience was greatly distressed. She now perceived that she had beguiled herself with prospects of a visionary nature; was entirely blinded to her own real character; had long placed her happiness in mere chimeras, and grounded her vain hopes upon imaginary foundations… when upon the point of perishing, in her own apprehension, the words of Lady Margaret returned strongly to her recollection, and she felt an earnest desire, renouncing every other hope, to cast herself wholly upon Christ for life and salvation. From her bed, she lifted up her heart to the Saviour, with this important prayer, and immediately all her distress and fears were removed, and she was filled with peace and joy in believing.' Not only that, but her health improved dramatically.

From the day of her conversion in July 1739, the Countess of Huntingdon was a changed woman. Interestingly, although we are not told that she objected to the new type of preaching before her conversion experience, it is recorded that, 'All offences at the Gospel plan of salvation died away,' and that, 'The stubbornness of the will was broken, and changed into a passive acquiescence in the sovereign will of God.' And the year surrounding her conversion was certainly one in which a passive acquiescence in the sovereign will of God would have been much needed for it was not an easy one for Selina.

Lady Betty, the stalwart of the family and Selina's mentor, was somewhat taken aback by the turn of events that found her sisters and sister-in-law changed women. Not only that, the Earl of Huntingdon himself seemed similarly affected, as 'the Scriptures are become his whole study.' Although she was suffering from cancer – or perhaps because she was – Lady Betty determined to put things back to rights again. Religion had its place in her life, after all it was she who had invited Ingham to preach in her chapel, but she seems to have felt that it should be kept in its place. By way of moderating the situation she wrote to Selina suggesting that she correspond with her friend Rev Thomas Barnard, who was also tutor to one of the Huntingdon's sons. Respectful of her sister-in-law, Selina accepted her advice though she did not go on to accept Barnard's counsel. His suggestions that Christians should not pray too much or be over zealous, that they should neither change their lifestyle nor take on spiritual commitments, did not meet with much favour in Donnington Park. It is little wonder that we see Selina's letters to Barnard tailing off after just a few months. There is probably no better testimony to the profound change in Selina Huntingdon than the fact she was prepared to disagree, albeit very graciously, with Lady Betty Hastings, whose love and acceptance meant so much to her.

The Methodists

Lady Margaret read Selina's mind more accurately and requested that her friend Benjamin Ingham (whom she was later to marry) should visit the Huntingdons and educate them from the Scriptures. At this point it might be helpful to consider where these preachers fitted in. They were known as Methodists, though that title was not new; it had been used in a derogatory way of the Pietists of a previous generation, and it was still a derogatory term. The Methodists of the 1730s included John and Charles Wesley, Benjamin Ingham, George Whitefield and Howell Harris, men who had formed the Holy Club in Oxford. Their preaching stressed three main points: firstly, everyone was a sinner and good works alone could not redeem; secondly, the abandonment of 'reason' and complete submission to God; and thirdly, the joy of a revelation of personal salvation.

The English preachers who became known as Methodists did not set out to establish a denomination, rather they sought to preach the gospel in order that souls would be saved and remain as salt and light in the Established Church. It happened that some independent groups did spring up, and that Methodism did become a denomination, but that was not the intention of the men who preached 'Methodism' in the 1730s.

Those who agreed with the Methodist preachers saw them as God's gift to the churches because they hoped that revival would come through them. And revival was much talked about because news of the results of Jonathan Edwards' preaching in Northampton, Massachusetts, came across the Atlantic with his A Narrative of Surprising Conversions, and by word of mouth from the Holy Club preachers who visited America. Those who disagreed with their Biblical teaching viewed them as ranters and ravers setting out to establish what they would describe as a cult. They certainly saw no place for them within the Established Church. Nor did the 1730s Methodists have a clearly defined theology. Among them were men of Arminian persuasion, the Wesleys among them, and others, like George Whitefield, who were Calvinists. The main points of their preaching allowed for both.

By aligning themselves with the Methodist preachers, Theophilus and Selina set themselves up to be laughed at and ridiculed. One of those happy to oblige in that department was her young sister Mary, who by then was back in England and in receipt of society gossip. It was in great high dudgeon that she wrote to Selina in the following terms (of Lady Margaret): 'that sect Is so Generally exploded that It's become a Joke of all

Compagnys, and Indeed I Can goe no whare but I hear of the uncommon piety of the Donnington family … I'm Conserned to think my Dear Sister who Is so reasonable In every thing Else should Encourage such a Cantting set of people.' But it was Lady Margaret who had the measure of Selina, and her suggestion that Benjamin Ingham spend some time at Donnington Park met with approval and the Huntingdons greatly benefited from his systematic teaching and preaching.

Within a few months two events happened that must have had a profound effect on the Countess. The year prior to her conversion Lady Betty was diagnosed as having breast cancer. She had surgery (one shudders at the thought of what that must have been like in the first half of the 18th Century) and it looked as though the disease had been prevented from spreading. But the cancer returned and it was clear that the much-respected lady did not have long to live. So right at the outset of her Christian life Selina had to practise the 'passive acquiescence in the sovereign will of God' that her relation noted.

A Much Fitter Ornament

There was another emotional upheaval to follow when her mother died in France, not long after making it known that she had 'cast off' all her

children. Their relationship must have been a sore
trial to the young Christian, one in which her
comfort would be in God's word, 'If it is possible, as
far as it depends on you, live at peace with everyone'
(Romans 12:18). And it seems that when the end
came there was a forgiving and peace-loving heart
in Selina. While Mary inherited from her mother's
will, nothing at all was left to the Countess. In
fact, when the estate was wound up there was not
enough in it to pay the legacies. It is a mark of
a changed woman that Selina along with Mary
(the third sister had died six years earlier) took it
upon themselves to finance the legacies. Mary was
left a diamond cross which she gave to her sister
as it was 'a much fitter ornament for you whose
Conduct on this occasion has so justly deserved
it' (from a letter from Lady Mary Kilmorey to
Lady Huntingdon). While she objected to the
fanaticism she associated with those who followed
the teaching of the Methodist preachers, it seems
that Mary had to acknowledge the Christian spirit
in which Selina dealt with their mother's final
arrangements. Before leaving the subject of her
changed life, it is encouraging to note that when,
in November 1740, one of the Countess's maids
was asked about her mistress's temper, the woman
assured the questioner that Selina had not been in
a passion for more than twelve months. That must

have been both a relief to the Donnington Park household and a fine witness to the Countess of Huntingdon's saving faith.

Astute and Generous

Looking back over the centuries it is clear that God was at that time raising up a remarkable group of preachers. Not only that, he was also raising up supporters through whom their work could be advanced, the Countess of Huntingdon among them. For a time in the early 1740s she lent her support to Charles and John Wesley. But following the deaths of two of her sons in 1743, and her husband in 1746, she found comfort in Calvinist theology rather than in what the Wesleys preached. Selina's early widowhood was marked by her increasing support of Howell Harris and George Whitefield rather than the Wesley brothers. Throughout the 1750s she gave financial assistance both to students and those in the ministry, as well as supporting in practical ways and through her influence in society. She was an astute woman, and when she realised that as a peeress she could build chapels on to property her family owned she was not slow to do so, particularly where they might reach out to people of her own social class whom she recognised as spiritually needy. All buildings other than those inside the Established Church needed to be licensed as dissenting places of worship apart from private chapels. The Countess was by then treading a fine line. It was her stated aim to encourage new life in the Established Church rather than form another denomination. However, her willingness to build private chapels – which were, in effect, Calvinistic Methodist churches – was really a step in the direction in which she did not want to go, had she but realised it.

In 1768 the wedge between her position and the Church of England was driven deeper when six ministerial students under her patronage were expelled from St Edmund Hall in Oxford. The Countess, encouraged by Howell Harris, established a college at Trevecca in South Wales. The foundation of the college coincided with the deepening of a theological rift that threatened the ministers she supported. Trevecca was also put under pressure by the impatience of its patron. Having set up an institution in which students for the ministry could devote themselves to study, the Countess of Huntingdon was so impatient to spread the gospel that she insisted on the students preaching so often they had little time to study at all! That kind of impatience seems to have been typical of Selina, and although she was no longer referred to as having a choleric temper, she was undoubtedly a passionate and volatile woman. When she eventually moved to Spa Fields in London and opened a chapel there the matter came to a head and the Countess of Huntingdon Connexion seceded from the Church of England. Sadly, Selina dominated all that she patronised, including the Connexion, and the matter of succession became a concern as she grew older. Eventually in 1790 she was persuaded to make arrangements for four friends to lead the Connexion after her death. That decision was not taken too soon for she died the following year.

Selina, Countess of Huntingdon had a remarkable place in the history of the church in England. She was willing and able to support those who felt hemmed in by the establishment and unable to preach the gospel. Her patronage was vast, extending to many, many clergymen and students who held to her evangelical viewpoint. It could be argued that without her the Wesleyans and Calvinistic Methodists would have taken much longer to establish than they did. Although she was undoubtedly a powerful woman who knew how to use her power, she was also an intensely private person as anyone who sets out to write her biography soon finds out. Selina's great vision was not of personal fame, rather it was the evangelisation of England first then the rest of the world. Interestingly, although the

Countess of Huntingdon Connection today is but a small group of congregations, they still do have a missionary interest in Africa.

It is extraordinary but true that God can take the most unlikely circumstances and use them to his glory. That is certainly true in Selina's case. She brought into her marriage a great deal of what today would be called baggage from her childhood: almost total breakdown of her wider family, dysfunctionality in her immediate family, financial stringency, rows and ructions over money, court cases that extended over generations and the famous temper. These combined to produce a strong and serious young woman and a good manager, one who could have balanced books much less well-endowed than those of the wealthy Huntingdons. Her mother leaving home when she was just six years old no doubt helped produce the strong-minded individual that Selina became. Her happy marriage and comfortable relationship with the extended Huntingdon family was God's gift to her after the long years of unhappiness. It allowed her to channel her hard experiences in positive directions, even more so when she and her husband were converted.

Having been reared frugally, for want of money rather than on any principle, she sat lightly on her wealth and was more than generous with it. Her management skills not only helped make up for her husband's total lack of them, but also allowed her to manage the college at Trevecca and the many churches she established. The wheeling and dealing that must have marked her childhood was redeemed for service later when, using a loophole in the law that allowed private chapels to be set up without licences, Selina effectively established missions to the upper classes in several of the spa towns of England. Even her choleric temper was called into service, because it most often manifested itself as passion, and Selina, the Countess of Huntingdon, could only have achieved what she achieved by being passionate about what she believed was for the Christian good of England and beyond.

5

Jonathan Edwards

The young Jonathan Edwards must have grown up aware of his heritage, and it still makes interesting reading today. His grandfather, Richard Edwards, had his roots in Wales. He was a Christian minister cum schoolmaster, and he and his wife Ann had a son named William. Richard died young and his widow married James Coles, who was also a Christian. The couple set out with William for a new life in America in the mid 1620s hoping that there they would have freedom to engage in the 'pure worship of the Lord Jesus Christ.' William, who became a cooper, married and produced a son Richard in 1647, the first of the Edwards to be born in New England. That gave him a unique place in his family's history. In time his son, Timothy, wrote an account of Richard's life. And it was Timothy who fathered Jonathan, the subject of this study. Jonathan's mother, Esther, was the daughter of Solomon Stoddart, one of the best-known clergymen in the new world. Her maternal grandfather was also a minister. Consequently,

Jonathan Edwards was a third generation New Englander, with a long Christian tradition on both sides of the family.

His home was in East Windsor where his father ministered for all of his working life. Jonathan was born there in 1703, no doubt much to the delight of his four older sisters. He was something of an odd one out in the family as he was followed by a further six sisters. When they were grown up the girls measured an amazing total of 60 feet, as each of them was six feet tall! Children did not come any cheaper then than they do now, and there was a constant struggle to provide for them. Their father eked out his stipend by working the land that came with the parsonage. Providing for his family was a very hands-on affair for him. Not only did he farm but he took in pupils too. In fact, the parsonage became a school of some note in the area. Two other people were almost members of the family. They were Mercy Brooks and Tim Demming, the Edwards' servants.

Despite her upbringing, and the fact that her husband would probably not have married her had she been an unbeliever, Esther Edwards did not make a profession of faith until Jonathan was in his teenage years. It is likely that she was one of those Christians who, lacking a sense of assurance, felt unable to come to the communion table. If that was the case she joins many today who deprive themselves of the sacramental blessings of the believer by not obeying the Lord's command to take and eat, remembering his death as they do so. Whatever the reason for Esther's reticence to profess faith, there is nothing in the family history to suggest either that she was an unbeliever during Jonathan's childhood or that she had a conversion experience when he was a teenager.

From an early age Jonathan Edwards was fascinated by nature. In later years he remembered back to spending many boyhood hours each August and September lying on the ground watching the abundance of butterflies and moths that lived in the area around his home. Just before his eighth birthday his father was drafted to serve as a chaplain to the Connecticut troops who were called up to deal with an invasion that was part of the Queen Anne's War. That must have affected the boy greatly, for not only did his father depart the family home for the first time, but he did so to go to a battlefield. No doubt the boy's mind ran through a whole riot of possible outcomes, including that his father might not return and he would be the 'man' of the house. Timothy's mind, however, ran along quite a different track and his letters home to Esther give his thoughts concerning his young family at home in East Windsor.

Timothy was concerned about their safety. 'If any of the children should at any time go over the river to a meeting, I would have them be exceeding careful how they sit or stand on the boat less they should fall into the river. … I wouldn't have thee venture him (Jonathan) to ride out into the woods with Tim.' He was no less concerned about their behaviour. 'I hope thou wilt take special care of Jonathan that he don't learn to be rude and naughty, etc., of which thee and I have lately discoursed.' Then there was the matter of education. 'Take care that Jonathan doesn't lose what he hath learned but that as he hath got the Accidence, and above two sides of propria quae moribus by heart so that he keep what he hath got.' He went on to suggest that one way of retaining Latin in Jonathan's memory until his father returned was to have the boy recite passages to his sisters 'pretty often'. Something of the spiritual measure of the man can be gleaned from the end of the same letter. 'The Lord Jesus Christ be with thy spirit, my Dear, and encourage thee to hope and trust in him, and discover his love to thy soul to whom I commit thee and all thine and mine, to whom remember my love, and also to Mercy Brooks and Tim Demming … and tell my children that I would have them to pray daily for their Father, and for their own souls, and above all things to remember their Creator and seek after the Lord Jesus Christ now in the days of their youth. God be with and bless you all. I am, my Dear, ever thine in the dearest love and affection, Timo: Edwards.' Not only does Timothy's letter tell us something of the spiritual concern of a father for his children, and his care about the practicalities of their lives, but it is written in such a loving and affectionate tone that we must conclude that the home was a contented and happy one.

Thoughts of death must have entered Jonathan's mind at that time as his father does not seem to have avoided the subject. 'I still have strong hopes of seeing thee and our dear children again,' he wrote some time later. 'I cannot but hope that I have had the gracious presence of God with me since I left home, encouraging and strengthening my soul, as well as preserving my life.' He went on to say that he trusted in the Lord to have mercy on all the family and that there was work still for him to do back home in East Windsor. Lest we think that Jonathan, the only son, was a favourite, when his father sent the children greetings towards the end of that letter their names: Esther, Elizabeth, Anne, Mary, Jonathan, Eunice, Abigail and Jerusha, are given in birth order. 'The Lord have mercy on and eternally save them all,' concluded Timothy. These letters to Esther paint a good picture of a fine home. Timothy did return after a severe illness invalided him out of service.

The Soldier's Return

Normal schooling resumed on Timothy Edward's return, though it is clear from his reference to Jonathan's Latin that it did not cease while he was away. The clergyman cum schoolmaster took his duties seriously. As well as teaching his own children, his seven Stoughton nephews along with some village boys were taught in the parsonage. And a very good job he made of their education, because those of his students who went on to college stood out against the others. One thing on which he was very strict was writing, insisting that whatever the children were reading or observing they did it with pen in hand to take notes. And these notes were not scrappy affairs, as he regarded accuracy of writing as essential.

Jonathan was an able student and often surprised his father with research he undertook on his own. On one occasion he presented Timothy with a sheaf of papers, the top one bearing the title, 'Of Insects.' 'Multitudes of times I have beheld with wonderment and pleasure the spiders marching in the air from one tree to another,' he had written, 'their little shining webs and Glistening Strings of a Great Length and at such a height as that one could think they were tack'd to the Sky by one end were it not that they were moving floating.' So accurate were the boy's observations that 'Of Insects' was preserved and acknowledged by the scientists of his day and thereafter. Jonathan applied what he had been taught of the Christian faith to his study of insects because he explained that the spiders' movements were caused not only by air currents and the changing seasons but also by the laws of nature 'operating in the eternal intention God had for the universe from the beginning of time.' The letter that accompanied his research project must have brought a smile to his father's face.

'Forgive me, sir, that I Do not Conceal my name, and Communicate this to you by a mediator. If you think the Observations Childish, and besides the Rules of Decorum, — with Greatness and Goodness overlook it in a Child & Conceal Sir, Although these things appear very Certain to me, yet Sir, I submit it all to your better Judgment & Deeper insight. . . . Pardon if I thought it might at Least Give you Occasion to make better observations, on these wondrous animals, that should [be] worthy of Communicating to the Learned world, respecting these wondrous animals, from whose Glistening Webs so much of the wisdom of the Creator shines. Pardon Sir

your most Obedient humble servant,

Jonathan Edwards

The faithful instruction the lad received from his parents rendered him when still a child 'familiarly conversant with the things of God'. He was made aware of his own sinful character and his duty to repent and seek forgiveness, and also of the new life that would begin in him at conversion and be continued and perfected in heaven. Jonathan had times when the Lord seemed to be drawing him towards himself. The first was when still a boy at home, and as he went to college when he was just thirteen years old; he was still a boy when he left home. There was a time of great spiritual awakening in his father's congregation and he was among those who seemed to be affected. For many months he was deeply concerned about his soul's salvation, praying five times a day alone as well as meeting up with some other boys who were of the same mind. They not only prayed together but spent 'much time in religious talk.' He and his friends found a swampy place and there they built a den where they gathered for prayer. When on his own Jonathan had a secret place of prayer in the wood near his home. During his times of prayer there he was 'from time to time much affected.' Years later, when taking a critical look at that experience in his childhood, he concluded that he did not know what kind of delight he had taken in religion, but that it had certainly involved 'much self-righteous pleasure.' He was a tenderhearted boy whose feelings were easily roused, and because of the Christian home in which he was reared his feelings deceived him into thinking they were the real thing. Later, realising what had happened to him then did not bring him to a saving faith made Jonathan aware that 'many are deceived with such affections, and such a kind of delight as I then had in religion, and mistake it for grace.'

The Sovereignty of God

Jonathan, however, did not just accept what he was told at home or mindlessly believe what his father preached in church. From quite a young age he had a real problem with the doctrine of God's sovereignty. It seemed to him 'a horrible doctrine' that God should choose some and not others, so condemning them to being 'everlastingly tormented in hell.' There were no doubt some interesting discussions between father and son in the East Windsor parsonage! In his Memoirs Jonathan recalls that his 'domestic circle was a scene of supplication, and it was a scene of instruction' and the supplication was perhaps redoubled when he raised doubts such as he had on the sovereignty of God.

There must have been a great deal of joy in the Edwards' home in 1715-16 when his mother and two of his sisters made professions of faith during a second time of blessing in the area. One of Jonathan's sisters, Mary, had left home by then and he wrote to tell her news of the blessings. 'Through the wonderful mercy and goodness of God there hath in this place been a very remarkable stirring and pouring out of the Sprit of God, and likewise now is, but I think I have reason to think it is in some measure diminished but I hope not much. About thirteen have been joined to the Church in an estate of full communion. … I think there comes commonly on Mondays above thirty persons to speak with Father about the condition of their souls.' He was twelve years old when he wrote that, and it is the earliest piece of his writing to survive. From what he tells us later in his life's story Jonathan was not a Christian at the time, but like so many pastors' children he knew the right words and how to use them; he no doubt thought that he meant them.

Just a few months later, in September 1716, Jonathan Edwards left East Windsor for college. He was all of twelve years and eleven months old. We have no reason to suppose that he left other than with a childish faith in God. Although Timothy Edwards had studied at Harvard, he thought it was beginning to stray from its evangelical foundation, which was why he sent his son to the more local Collegiate School of Connecticut, which was soon to become Yale. Founded in 1702, the College was little older than Jonathan himself. Enshrined in the its charter was the need for twice daily prayer to be taken by the rector, practical theology to be taught each Sunday, and all teaching to be compatible with the Westminster Confession of Faith. A quotation from the Orders and Appointments of the College gives us an idea where it stood. 'Every student shall exercise himself in reading Holy Scriptures by himself every day … All students shall avoid the profanation of God's holy name, attributes, Word and ordinances and the Holy Sabbath, and shall carefully attend all public assemblies for divine worship. … All undergraduates shall publically repeat sermons in the hall …' But while the foundation of the course was sound, the College had no actual foundations because it didn't have a building at all! As the rector also had a congregation to care for, the students at first lived in his own home or nearby. But as student numbers grew and other members of staff were engaged, the need for a permanent building became an issue that could no longer be avoided. Necessity, however, did not make the choice of a site easy and for a time students were split into two groups based in different locations. In fact, Jonathan was just ten miles from home at

New Haven. The other part of the College was at Wethersfield.

The course Jonathan Edwards followed was the same as his father had taken in Harvard, so much so that he was able to use the same texts. Lasting four years, in the first year students did mainly Latin, Greek and Hebrew. Logic filled most of the second year, natural science the third, and arithmetic with geometry and astronomy the final year. After a difficult period in the life of the College – and nothing whatever to do with Jonathan! – Timothy wrote to the master. He, in his reply, congratulated Timothy on his son's 'promising abilities and advances in knowledge.' Although Jonathan was obviously doing well at College, attending prayers twice daily, reciting the Westminster Confession with the whole student body every Saturday night, and learning practical theology Sunday by Sunday, things were not well with his soul. His convictions became less convincing, and his affection for the Lord dulled with the passage of time. Jonathan reached a stage at which he could say 'I entirely lost all those affections and delights.' He stopped the practice of private prayer, or at least the desire for prayer ceased to move him.

Towards the end of his time at college Jonathan was at peace with neither himself nor with God, and it took a severe and painful bout of pleurisy to bring him to his senses. At the peak of his illness he reckoned that God 'brought me nigh to the grave, and shook me over the pit of hell.' No doubt that threw him into a prayerful state of mind, but only for a time. Before long he had drifted back into his godless ways but the experience had rendered his conscience tender and the Lord gave him no peace. Jonathan had many inward struggles with outward temptations before he came to a point where he felt he had no choice but to change his ways. Making a vow to the Lord, he was moved to leave his 'wicked ways' and avoid temptation whenever he could, and resist it when he could not avoid it. He set himself a programme of spiritual duties and stuck to it, but there was no warmth or delight in anything he did and none of the heartfelt fervour he had known as a child in his den in the woods.

Spending much time in introspection only brought further struggles that seemed to take him nowhere. Jonathan decided that he would apply himself to seeking salvation and make that the focal point of his life until he should find it. But doing that landed him in such a miserable state that nothing seems to have been gained. His 'concern continued, and prevailed, with many exercising thoughts and inward struggles; but yet it never seemed to be proper, to express that concern by the name of terror.' Jonathan Edwards was one very unhappy young man. And his unhappiness must have deepened when he suffered the death of his grandfather, Richard Edwards, especially as that was the first time death had struck at his near family. It would have been particularly sad for Jonathan as his grandfather lived near the College and he would have seen him regularly. In the passing, it must be noted that it was most unusual at that time for a boy to reach his teens without meeting death in the family. Death was a much commoner visitor to young families then than it is now, and for the Edwards to have escaped is quite remarkable. Esther Edwards, in fact, lived to be ninety two years of age!

Graduation and Beyond

Despite his inner turmoil Jonathan acquitted himself well at College and finished as the highest-ranking student in the Bachelor of Arts Degree course. As such he was privileged to deliver the Farewell Address on graduation day, which was actually the first day of the autumn term rather than the final day of the previous one. Having done three years at New Haven he remained there for a further two to obtain his Master of Arts in Divinity. We have no reason to suppose that his spiritual state was much changed when he began his post-graduate degree, though he does seem to have been aware of his lifelessness. Little remains that he wrote at that time to enlighten us. However, in his Memoir, Jonathan goes straight from describing his confusion and despair to recalling his childhood problems with the doctrine of the sovereignty of God. It seems possible that God's sovereignty had become part of his problem. It may be that because he sought salvation but did not seem to find it, he began to doubt that he was among the elect. That would certainly have added to his distress. But whether it was then or later, the doctrinal issue was eventually resolved and his mind was enlightened on the subject. 'I remember the time very well,' he wrote years later, 'when I seemed to be convinced and fully satisfied, as to this sovereignty of God, and his justice in thus eternally disposing of men, according to his sovereign pleasure. But never could give an account how, or by what means, I was thus convinced, but in the least imagining at the time, nor a long time after, that there was any extraordinary influence of God's Spirit in it; but only that now I saw further, and my reason apprehended the justice and reasonableness to it. However, my mind rested in it; and it put an end to all those cavils and objections.' The subject was never a problem to Jonathan after that, so much so that the doctrine became to him 'exceedingly pleasant, bright, and sweet.' What a relief that must have been to his father.

It had been years since Jonathan had used the words sweet and delightful to describe his spiritual experience, and then it had turned out to be a childish and surface sweetness and a premature delight, but those were the words he used of his new experience. It happened one day as he read from Scripture, 'Now unto the King eternal, immortal, invisible, the only wise God, be honour and glory for ever and ever. Amen (1 Tim. 1:17 KJV). As he read the words a sense of God's glory flooded his soul in quite a different way than he had ever experienced before. Never in the past had Scripture had that effect on him. His mind and heart were full of the excellency of God and he knew that his greatest happiness – his only happiness – was to be found in the enjoyment of God. The young man's soul yearned to be held in that state of glory until it could be taken to heaven and there enjoy an even deeper sense of the glory of the Lord. Repeating the words he had read over and over again it was as though they became the song that his heart was singing. And his song led him to prayer of a kind quite different from the formality that prayer had become. His prayer time was warm and full of his heart's affection. 'But it never came into my thought,' he wrote in his Memoir of that experience, 'that there was anything spiritual, or of a saving nature, in this.'

From that time on Jonathan Edwards became much more spiritually aware. He often found his mind wandering to the subject of the person of Christ, to the work of redemption wrought through his death of the cross, and to the way of salvation thus opened. He does not say that he was by then converted, but his oppressive conviction of sin was lifted from him as he experienced a new enjoyment of God, because he went on to say, 'An inward, sweet sense of these things, at times, came into my heart; and my soul was led away in pleasant views and contemplations of them. And my mind was greatly engaged to spend my time in reading and meditating on Christ, on the beauty and excellency of his person, and the lovely way of salvation by free grace in him.' A reader from boyhood, Jonathan's pleasure now lay in books about the Lord. And the words that wove themselves into his mind were those from Canticles 2, 'I am the rose of Sharon, and the lily of the valleys.' These lovely expressions seemed to him to catch the beauty of the Lord. The concerns of the world that had burdened him dissolved and his thoughts were of altogether higher things. The imagination that had so recently been disturbed by thoughts of death and hell now pictured high mountains, wide wildernesses and other such isolated and beautiful places, and always in the midst of the loveliness of the vision Jonathan pictured himself talking alone with Jesus. The words he uses to describe these months are words of love, words that could only have come from sins forgiven and a heart renewed.

Not long after this he spent some time discussing things with his father. One can imagine Timothy wondering what course their talk would take, whether it would be based yet again on the doctrine of the sovereignty of God and his son's serious misgivings about it. What a joyful surprise it must have been for him to find that problem had been consigned to the past and that Jonathan was aglow with a new joy and peace. The time they spent together would have been precious to his father, but it was also precious to Jonathan. 'I gave an account to my father of some things that had passed in my mind. I was pretty much affected by the discourse we had together.' Having shared what was in his heart, Jonathan took himself out for a walk. As he looked up to the clouds in the sky he was suddenly filled with a sense of God's majesty and grace, such that he struggled to find words to express it. 'It was a sweet, and gentle, and holy majesty; and also a majestic meekness; an awful sweetness; a high, and great, and holy gentleness.'

Time passed and Jonathan developed more of a sense of divine things, and enjoyed an inner sweetness that he had never experienced before. As he looked around him it seemed that he was seeing things with new eyes. He would have well understood the hymn writer who wrote:

> *Heaven above is softer blue,*
> *Earth around is sweeter green;*
> *Something lives in every hue,*
> *Christless eyes have never seen:*
> *Birds with gladder songs o'erflow,*
> *Flowers with deeper beauties shine,*
> *Since I know, as now I know,*
> *I am his, and he is mine.'*
>
> (George Wade Robinson)

A Changed Life

As Jonathan looked around him it seemed that God's excellency, wisdom, purity and love appeared in everything he saw, all of creation appeared to be speaking of its maker. As astronomy was one of his third-year subjects he would have been well used to looking at the night sky, but now he found himself sitting for long periods of time gazing at the moon just for the enjoyment of knowing the One who made it. During the day he often lay watching the clouds scudding across the sky, intensely aware that they were just a tiny reflection of the glory of God, and that the sun that beat down on him was dark compared to the light of Jesus Christ. Sometimes he was struck to silence by the awe of it all, but often he found himself 'singing forth, with a low voice, my contemplations of the Creator and Redeemer.'

Of all the wonders of creation that he enjoyed so deeply at that time, nothing thrilled Jonathan Edwards more that a thunderstorm, and this was in stark contrast to how they affected him previously. Not so long before he was 'uncommonly terrified' by thunder and lightning, but that changed when he changed. 'At the first appearance of a thunderstorm (I) used to take the opportunity ... to fix myself in order to view the clouds, and see the lightnings play, and hear the majestic and awful voice of God's thunders ... leading me to sweet contemplation of my great and glorious God.' Once again Jonathan tells us that he sang his thoughts as the thunder rolled round the hills and the lightning flashed above his head. One wonders what effect the great change in his life had on his college contemporaries and friends, because the man he was before the experience that so completely changed him did not sound like one who sang his way through his days, far less through a thunderstorm.

Jonathan Edwards at that time experienced deep spiritual joy, and the more he meditated on the greatness of God the more he sought after holiness. So vehement was his longing for holiness that his heart 'seemed to be full and ready to break.' He could easily identify with the psalmist, 'My soul is weary with sorrow; strengthen me according to your word' (Ps. 119:28). The sorrow he knew was a sorrow over sin, and what he longed for was more of God's strong holiness. This argues against any thought that Edwards was caught up in some kind of sentimental and ecstatic experience. Often his heart was overwhelmed with sadness that he had not turned to Christ sooner than he did, especially considering the privileges of his Christian home and godly upbringing. Had he come to Christ as a child, he reasoned, he would now be further along the road to holiness because he would have had more time to grow in grace.

It was Jonathan's delight to be alone in the beauty of creation where he could meditate, 'converse with God and … sing forth (his) contemplations.' Prayer, he said, came naturally to him then because it gave vent to what was in his 'burning heart'. Twice before, as a boy, he seemed to burn for the Lord, but what he now experienced was altogether different. He compared his experiences in the following words. 'The delights which I now felt in the things of religion, were of an exceeding different kind from those ... I had when a boy; and what then I had not more notion of, than one born blind has of pleasant and beautiful colours. They were of a more inward, pure, soul-animating, and refreshing nature. Those former delights never reached the heart; and did not arise from any sight of the divine excellency of the things of God; or any taste of the soul-satisfying and life-giving good there was in them.'

In his Memoir Jonathan Edwards says that he spent most of his time thinking of divine things year after year. He doesn't state to which years he refers and there are disagreements regarding the date of his conversion. Harold Simonson in Jonathan Edwards, *Theologian of the Heart*, dates it to January 1723, by which time Jonathan was nineteen years old and halfway through his first ministry in New York. But Iain H Murray in his Jonathan Edwards, *A New Biography* suggests that it took place in 1721 while he was still a student. It is difficult to read his Memoirs, quoted above, and relating to the last year and a half of his college education, and not accept that they are the sentiments of a young man who was well and truly converted. Simonson bases his date on a quotation from Edward's 'Personal Narrative' dated 12th January 1723, in which he said, 'I make a solemn dedication of myself to God, and wrote it down; giving myself, and all that I had, to God; to be for the future in no respect my own; to act as one that has no right to himself, in any respect.' However, in the light of what had gone before, it would seem that this marked an act of rededication rather than his conversion.

Having finally completed his education Jonathan Edwards was invited to supply a small Presbyterian church in New York and he served there for eight months, from August 1722 until April 1723. Towards the end of his college years he began to write down resolutions he made and he continued to note them in his diary when in New York. In a resolution dated 18th December 1722 we gain some insight into his conversion experience and, from his point of view, its deficiencies. He did not remember that he 'experienced regeneration, exactly in those steps, in which divines say it is generally wrought.' His conversion is a fine example of God dealing with individuals individually. Of his time in New York Jonathan noted that he had spent it in 'sweet and pleasant days', but there had also been some days that were neither sweet nor pleasant. For example, in January he complained of experiencing a long dullness about reading the Scriptures and of enduring a time of listlessness. Considering his state he concluded that 'Sin is not enough mortified. Without the influences of the Spirit of God, the old serpent would begin to rouse up himself from his frozen state.' That brought about yet another resolution – that he had been negligent in not striving enough in duty and not forcing himself to think religious thoughts. But lest we think that had become his normal state, two days later he recorded in his diary that he had higher thoughts than usual of the excellency of Christ and that had resulted in an unusual repentance of sin. Jonathan Edwards was certainly an exceptional man, but he was a mere man with normal ups and downs. An interesting note appears in his diary for 2nd May 1723, the afternoon after he returned home from New York. He recorded that when he meditated in New York he imagined himself walking in the fields of East Windsor, but on return there he discovered himself imagining he was walking in the fields of New York. It must be a very long time since anyone walked in New York's elysian fields!

The Northampton Years

The following year the young man's gifts were recognised and Jonathan Edwards was invited to be senior tutor at Yale, which meant he would effectively be head of the College. He might well have remained there had he not been asked to become colleague and successor to his grandfather, Solomon Stoddart, in Northampton, Massachusetts. On 15th February 1727, when he was twenty four years old, the young man was ordained and began working alongside his very well-known grandfather, a man of much zeal and huge personality. After settling in Northampton, Jonathan married Sarah Pierpont and established a home that was to become legendary as a haven of happy family life. Having benefited from a joyful childhood he provided for his children to have the same.

Although there were quite serious theological differences between Jonathan and his grandfather, they served the Lord together until Solomon Stoddart's death in 1929. During Stoddart's ministry there had been several times of revival in the congregation. After his death the Holy Spirit continued to come in reviving power during Jonathan's ministry. In fact Northampton was well known for its 'awakenings'. At one point the congregation's membership included almost the entire population of the town. It was not, however, a united congregation. Stoddart had admitted to the Lord's Table those who made no profession of conversion. Jonathan acquiesced as long as his grandfather was alive, but set out to change things thereafter and that, from time to time, caused rumblings of dissent. However, in the main the thirteen to fifteen hours a day he spent in his study told in his preaching and there was great blessing. In 1735, nine years after going to Northampton, an awakening began in the church in which more than 300 people were converted, including a little girl who was just four years old. The whole Connecticut valley was aflame for the Lord and news of it spread far. Five years later, when George Whitefield the famous English preacher visited the area, there began another period of fervour that spread from place to place until churches throughout the land heard about it and many were affected by it. This Great Awakening is reckoned to be the historical highpoint of Christianity in the New World.

In 1750, while the Great Awakening was still fresh in people's memories, Northampton's old problem raised its head once more. There were still those who remained from his grandfather's ministry who came to the Lord's Supper even though they knew they were not converted. By then Jonathan was totally convinced of the wrongness of this practice, and of the danger these people put themselves in. 'For anyone who eats and drinks without recognising the body of the Lord eats and drinks judgment on himself' (1 Cor. 11:29).

He decided that two courses of action should be followed: those members who were not Christians should come under the discipline of the church, and greater care should be taken in receiving new applicants into membership. Despite all the blessings that had gone before, the outcome of this was that Jonathan Edwards was asked to resign the charge; the voting was 20 to 2.

Married and with a very large family – they eventually had eleven children – the Edwards were faced with what to do and where to go. God led Jonathan into quite a different area of service, as missionary of The Society in London for Propagating the Gospel in New England and the Parts Adjacent. This involved moving to Stockbridge where he became pastor to the twelve white families who lived there and missionary to the Housatonic Indians. Although from the beginning he was involved in weighty social matters, e.g. the corruption that prevented the Indians benefiting from the money that was designated for their good, he also wrote some of his most famous books. Edwards had written throughout his ministry in Northampton, and his works were well known, but it was in Stockbridge that he wrote his weighty tomes on original sin, free will, the nature of true virtue and the end for which God created the world. The seven years Jonathan Edwards spent in Stockbridge were probably the most fruitful of his ministry, though it is for the Great Awakening that he is best remembered.

In 1757 an invitation came to Edwards to become President of the College of New Jersey at Princeton. He agreed, but only after much prayer and heart searching and with a fair degree of reluctance. Princeton's claim on him was that it was from the same theological stable as his own college, and founded on principles with which he wholeheartedly agreed. Further, his friends to whom he looked for advice felt that he should accept the call and the challenge. The following January Edwards moved to Princeton to take up his new duties. Two or three weeks after arriving he had an inoculation against smallpox, a disease that was a real scourge at the time. In the providence of God, Jonathan Edwards contracted smallpox from the vaccine and died of the disease five weeks later. So ended the life of the man who was arguably America's greatest theologian, and so began that life that is far better for which he had longed from his birth in the Christian faith.

Advice to young converts

As a postscript to the story of Jonathan Edward's conversion there follows an abbreviated form of his Advice to Young Converts which began its life as part of a letter written to a young woman who had recently come to faith and who wrote to him for advice.

1. I would advise you to keep up as great a strife and earnestness in religion in all aspects of it, as you would do if you knew yourself to be in a state of nature and you were seeking conversion.

2. Don't slack off seeking, striving, and praying for the very same things that we exhort unconverted persons to strive for, and a degree of which you have had in conversion.

3. When you hear sermons, hear them for yourself even though what is spoken in them may be more especially directed to the unconverted or to those that in other respects are in different circumstances from yourself.

4. Though God has forgiven and forgotten your past sins, yet don't forget them yourself.

5. Remember that you have more cause, on some accounts, a thousand times more, to lament and humble yourself for sins that have been since conversion than those that were before conversion, because of the infinitely greater obligations that are upon you to live to God.

6. Be always greatly humbled by your remaining sin, and never think that you lie low enough for it, but yet don't be at all discouraged or disheartened by it.

7. When you engage in the duty of prayer, come to the sacrament of the Lord's Supper, or attend any other duty of divine worship, come to Christ as Mary Magdalene did.

8. Remember that pride is the worst viper that is in the heart, and greatest disturber of the soul's peace and sweet communion with Christ.

9. That you may pass a good judgment on your spiritual condition, always consider your best conversations and best experiences to be the ones that produce the following two effects: first, those conversations and experiences that make you least, lowest, and most like a little child; and, second, those that do most engage and fix your heart in a full and firm disposition to deny yourself for God and to spend and be spent for him.

10. If at any time you fall into doubts about the state of your soul under darkness and dull frames of mind, it is proper to look over past experiences.

11. When the exercise of grace is at a low ebb, and corruption prevails, and by that means fear prevails, don't desire to have fear cast out any other way than by the reviving prevailing of love …

12. You should be often exhorting and counseling and warning others …

13. When you counsel and warn others, do it earnestly, affectionately, and thoroughly.

14. If you would set up religious meetings of your women by yourselves, to be attended once in a while, besides the other meetings you attend, I should think it would be very proper and profitable.

15. Under special difficulties, or when in great need of or great longings after any particular mercies for your self or others, set apart a day of secret fasting and prayer alone.

16. Don't let the adversaries of religion have any grounds to say that these converts don't carry themselves any better than others.

17. Don't talk of things of religion and matters of experiences with an air of lightness and laughter, which is too much the custom in many places.

18. In all your course, walk with God and follow Christ as a little, poor, helpless child, taking hold of Christ's hand, keeping your eye on the mark of the wounds on his hands and side.

19. Pray much for the church of God and especially that he would carry on his glorious work that he has now begun. Be much in prayer for the ministers of Christ.

Jonathan Edward's childhood was spent in a busy, happy Christian home though that did not make him a believer. But it did teach him about home life and when he went on to marry and establish his own home he based it on the same principles and it became well known as a loving and joyful place. As a boy Jonathan was fascinated with the natural world in general, and insect life in particular. His nature studies were mature well beyond his years. When he left Northampton to live and work among the Housatonic Indians, his deep interest in natural things no doubt gave him points of contact with these people who were legendary for their knowledge of the environment in which they lived. Educated at home by his father, Jonathan learned rigid study discipline, and nothing could have stood him in better stead when the Lord's time came for him to write profound theological books in a house full of children.

As a boy, Jonathan thought he had a living faith until the Holy Spirit made it clear to him that it had just been an emotional experience. Years later, in the awakenings in Northampton, he was faced with many people – some of them children – who thought they had come to faith. His own experience must have helped his discernment regarding the genuineness of these conversions. Edwards grew to love the doctrine of the sovereignty of God, but only after a hard battle. There can be no doctrine more needful at a time of revival in order to keep a sense of perspective and a spirit of humility. He must have been grateful that his thinking on the subject was clear, even though it was hard won. God not only used Jonathan Edward's pre-conversion experiences, he also placed him at a point in the history of America when his biblical theology could be spread to maximum effect. The Great Awakening was not a short-lived local phenomenon, but one that left its mark on great swathes of America and for a very long time after the event.

6

Charles Spurgeon

When Charles Haddon Spurgeon was just a few months old his family moved from Kelvedon in Essex, where he was born in 1834, to Colchester. Just four months later the infant was on the move again, this time to his grandfather's home in Stambourne where he remained until he was nearly five years old. Why his parents did not bring Charles up in his early years is not at all clear, but the Lord certainly used his godly grandfather as an influence for good on his life. Rev James Spurgeon was a nonconformist minister, as was his son John, Charles's father. In his autobiography, Spurgeon tells an interesting story which confirms his grandparent's influence on his life. It seems that on their mantelshelf there was an object of much fascination to the boy. It was an apple held within a glass globe that was hardly bigger than the apple. Having examined the glass from every angle, young Charles discovered that the apple could not have gone in through the neck as it was much too narrow, nor did the bottom unscrew, and the glass seemed to be intact in every way. It was only when the summer came that he discovered the apple had not gone in by magic, as his young mind had concluded. Truth dawned when he looked at one of his grandfather's apple trees and saw an identical glass globe with an apple growing inside it. The apple had been put through the neck of the globe when it was small enough to go in easily and the glass was attached to the branch of the tree on which the fruit was growing. So by autumn, Charles realised, the fruit would have grown to fill the globe and it would stand as a great puzzle to some other child, but not to him. In his later years he wrote that he had been like that apple, he had been placed as a child where the Lord wanted him to grow and be nurtured in the faith.

Each Sunday morning Charles was sent into the parlour with James Spurgeon, and given the Evangelical Magazine to look at while his grandfather completed his sermon preparation. The magazine was intended to keep the boy quiet, but what really stilled him into comparative silence was the old man's explanation that if he didn't have peace to look over his sermon he wouldn't preach it well and some poor souls would not hear the gospel and would not go to heaven. That early exhortation was probably just meant to give the minister a time of quiet before the service, but it found its way into Charles's heart and remained there to disturb him until he was converted. The lad knew that heaven was reserved for Christians and he certainly did not want to be one of those who missed out on going there.

It was the custom to hold family prayers in the parsonage at Stambourne and the precocious Charles took his turn at reading Scripture. One incident shows that even as a small child he had an enquiring mind for the things of the Lord and a persistence that must have kept his grandparents on their toes. On that occasion the boy didn't understand the meaning of the verses he was given to read about the end times and final judgement, and his grandfather did not explain them. Charles was not to be deflected for he read the same verses every day at family worship, each time asking for an explanation, until his grandfather had no choice but give him one, and a graphic one at that. So the young Charles Spurgeon showed early signs of wanting to know exactly what God's Word was about, and making strenuous efforts to find out. But more than that, what his grandfather told him that day about the last judgement added to his concern about being one of those who would spend eternity in heaven ,and created in the child both a healthy fearfulness of hell and a longing to be one of God's people.

It was while he was at Stambourne that the young Charles Spurgeon fell in love with books, and that does not express it too strongly. One little room in the parsonage was a book storeroom and the boy was often to be found there in his 'gold-mine' when other boys his age would have been out kicking a ball around. The book that most satisfied and fascinated him was Pilgrim's Progress, an old illustrated edition that set his imagination on fire. On visits back to his grandfather's parsonage when he was older and living with his parents, invariably found him tucked in his gold-mine discovering treasure after treasure, especially stories of Christian martyrs and tales from church history. One memory of Stambourne that did not hugely impress Spurgeon when he thought back upon it in adulthood was the Sunday School teaching, though he did admit that the memory work he had done: scripture, verses of hymns and Dr Watt's Catechism were in themselves most valuable. Despite his age Charles attended a little day school for 'very juvenile' children from the age of four. His teacher had a son called Gabriel and Charles longed to meet the angelic being. When he did so and discovered a very ordinary young man he was not impressed!

Tearful Goodbye

The time came when James and Charles, the old and the young Spurgeons, had to part and the boy return to his parents. Lest it be thought his grandfather was a severe man only intent on frightening the child into becoming a Christian, let Charles dispel the idea with his recollection of their parting. 'It was the great sorrow of my little life. Grandfather seemed very sorry, too, and we had a cry together; he did not quite know what to say to me, but he said, "Now child, to-night, when the moon shines at Colchester, and you look at it, don't forget that it is the same moon as your grandfather will be looking at from Stambourne;" and for years, as a child, I used to love the moon because I thought that my grandfather's eyes and my own somehow met there on the moon.'

Although Charles' home became Colchester just before his fifth birthday he often went back to his grandparents. And it is an account from one such holiday that shows us that Charles, though deeply interested in the faith, was quite a normal boy. His grandmother, in an effort to encourage the lad to learn hymns by heart, offered him a penny for each one he memorised. So enthusiastic was he that she had to reduce that to a halfpenny, then a farthing. But when James Spurgeon mentioned that they were having a problem with rats in the parsonage and offered Charles a shilling for every dozen he caught and killed, his grandson abandoned learning hymns for the much more lucrative job of rat-catching!

When he was ten years old, and again at Stambourne, a prophecy was made that seemed most unlikely to come to pass. Richard Knill, of the London Missionary Society, was on deputation in the area and stayed with the Spurgeons. Taking note of young Charles he asked where the lad slept. At six o'clock the following morning the boy was wakened by a knock at his bedroom door. It was Knill inviting him to go for a walk in the garden with him. What happened there remained with Charles all his life. 'He told me of the love of Jesus, and of the blessedness of trusting in him and loving him in our childhood. With many a story he preached Christ to me, and told me how good God had been to him, and then he prayed that I might know the Lord and serve him. He knelt down in that arbour, and prayed for me... He heard my childish talk with patient love, and repaid it with gracious instruction. On three successive days he taught me, and prayed with me …' Before Knill left Stambourne, he took Charles on his knee and told those present, 'This child will one day preach the gospel, and he will preach it to great multitudes. I am persuaded that he will preach in the chapel of Rowland Hill.' Having prophesied that Charles would preach in the largest church in the country, Knill gave the boy sixpence to learn the hymn 'God moves in a mysterious way his wonders to perform,' and extracted from him a promise that when he was grown up and preached in Rowland Hill's chapel that hymn should be sung. That was an extraordinary experience for an impressionable ten–year–old, one that he had good reason to remember, especially many years later when Knill's prophecy was fulfilled.

Although Charles lived at home with his parents, brother and sisters, the childhood influences that he recorded have more to do with his grandparents than his parents. There is no suggestion at all that he was not happy at home, or that he didn't enjoy his siblings' company. But there must have been deep sadnesses to endure there, for although his parents produced eight children who lived through childhood, a further nine died in infancy. Perhaps that dark providence had something to do with Charles living with his grandparents for nearly the first five years of his life.

It may be that Charles' father John, who was also a nonconformist minister, was a stricter man in the boy's eyes than his grandfather, for the short accounts he gives of his time at home paint him in that light. In his autobiography he tells of buying a slate and chalk on credit with a view to paying the money from gifts he was sure he would receive at Christmas. The princely sum owed was a farthing. When his father heard of the deal, Charles was in receipt of a lecture that he long remembered. John 'did not intend to bring up his children to speculate, and play at what big rogues call financing, and therefore he knocked my getting into debt on the head at once, and no mistake. He gave me a very powerful lecture upon getting into debt, and how like it was to stealing, and upon the way in which people were ruined by it, and how a boy who would owe a farthing, might one day owe a hundred pounds, and get into prison, and his family into disgrace.' Strong stuff! Charles' comment on the affair shows no grudge was borne for the row he received. 'God bless him for it,' he wrote, 'he was a sensible man, and none of your children-spoilers.'

Gathered Round the Table

It seems that Charles's mother made as much, if not more of a spiritual impression on him than his father. It was her practice on Sunday evenings when her children were young enough not to attend the evening service, to gather them round the table and have them read a passage of scripture that she then explained verse by verse. That done 'there came a time of pleading' when she encouraged her children to place their faith in Jesus. Then to reinforce what she had said, she read from such books as Alleine's An Alarme to Unconverted Sinners and Baxter's Call to the Unconverted 'with pointed observations' to each of her children as she read. Having done all that she humanly could to fix her children's eyes on Jesus, she then prayed for them in words that ate their way into Charles's being. 'Now, Lord, if my children go on in their sins, it will not be from ignorance that they perish, and my soul must bear a swift witness against them at the day of judgement if they lay not hold of Christ.' The thought of his mother bearing witness against him hit Charles where it hurt, no doubt contributing to his very tender conscience.

Charles had a true awareness of sin from a young age. There were times when he sorrowed deeply over his sins, when 'day and night God's hand was heavy' upon him. In his dreams he was often taken back to his grandfather's description of the final judgement and he saw in his unconscious eye the bottomless pit. When he awoke from dreaming the feeling of misery evoked in him did not go away. And when these times of conviction were upon him he found little comfort in attending church services as his 'song was but a sigh.' Sometimes Charles resorted to his bedroom to weep his heart out over his sins. He felt as though God's law was flogging him 'with a two-pronged whip, and then rubbing ... with brine afterwards.'

No doubt such signs of spiritual awakening were welcomed by Spurgeon's parents as a sign that their prayers were being answered. According to him, they were godly people and very protective of what might bring their offspring into temptation. He and his siblings were 'watched with jealous eyes, scarcely ever permitted to mingle with questionable associates, warned not to listen to anything profane or licentious, and taught the ways of God …' Charles was also well aware of his mother's tears and his father's supplications on his behalf. Although he saw the change Christ had made in believers' lives, and although he was fearful of hell and reminded of the possibility of a lost eternity in his dreams as well as his waking hours, still the boy put off making an act of commitment. His parents surely redoubled their prayers for their eldest son as he seemed to waver on the brink. Like many children of Christian parents Charles did not find it easy to talk to his father and mother about his spiritual condition. 'When I was under concern of soul,' he wrote later, 'the last persons I should have elected to speak to upon religion would have been my parents.'

Having said that he could not speak to them, it is still clear that his parents left a lasting spiritual impression on the young Charles Spurgeon. It is easier to evaluate such things from a distance, and when he wrote his biography what he said of his mother was most moving. Admitting that he didn't have the power of speech to describe the blessing it was to have had a mother who prayed for him and with him, he went on to say that he would never forget the tears in her eyes when she warned him to escape from the wrath that was to come. 'Nor can her frown be effaced from my memory – that solemn, loving frown, when she rebuked my budding iniquities; and her smiles have never faded from my recollections – the beaming of her countenance when she rejoiced to see some good thing in me towards the Lord God of Israel.'

No doubt it was years after it happened that John Spurgeon shared one memory in particular with his son; and of all the incidents that are recorded about Charles' parents perhaps this is the most eloquent. John was travelling to preach away from home, as he often did, when he had a sudden conviction that he was caring for the souls of strangers and away so often that he was neglecting the souls of his very own children. Realising the serious consequences that could result from such neglect he turned and went right back home. There was no-one there to greet him, but as he climbed the stairs he heard a voice coming from his bedroom. He listened at the door and heard his wife pouring out her soul to the Lord on behalf of their children, especially Charles, their strong-willed older son. As John stood there he knew that his children were in safe hands while he was away preaching, so without even disturbing his wife's prayer he went down the stair, left the house and proceeded to his preaching engagement.

A Critical Listener

Living in a parsonage as he did, Charles sat under the preaching of God's Word week by week, though his father was not always the preacher. He was a critical listener. Of one series of sermons on the Epistle to the Hebrews he commented 'I wished frequently that the Hebrews had kept the Epistle to themselves, for it sadly bored one poor Gentile lad.' But it was not always so. He was very moved under one particularly powerful sermon. Thinking that the time had come to seek the Lord, he wrestled within himself and poured out his heart in prayer. That afternoon he went back to church hoping to be encouraged to take the step of faith that he knew was necessary, but the sermon was poor and did not commend Christ at all, leaving Charles confused and disheartened. Once again the moment and the opportunity passed. Remembering the despair of that day, he wrote 'I could not believe, I could not lay hold on Christ; I was shut out, if no-one else was.' And in those few words we can feel the pain that wounded him.

When Charles was fourteen years old he left home for a second time, but on this occasion he did not go alone. His young brother James, three years his junior, went with him to St Augustine's Church of England School in Maidstone, Kent. Within a short time of his going there Charles was to have a conversation that made a powerful impression on him and help mould his thinking on the subject of baptism.

'Clergyman: *What is your name?*

Spurgeon: *Spurgeon, Sir.*

Clergyman: *No, no; what is your name?*

Spurgeon: *Charles Spurgeon, Sir.*

Clergyman: *No, you should not behave ...so, for you know I only want your Christian name.*

Spurgeon: *If you please, Sir, I'm afraid I haven't got one.*

Clergyman: *Why, how is that?*

Spurgeon: *Because I do not think I am a Christian.*

Clergyman: *What are you then – a heathen?*

Spurgeon: *No, Sir; but we may not be heathens and yet be without the grace of God, and so not be truly Christians.*

Clergyman: *Well, well, never mind; what is your first name?*

Spurgeon: *Charles.*

Clergyman:	*Who gave you that name?*
Spurgeon:	*I'm sure I don't know, Sir; I know no godfather ever did anything for me, for I never had any. Likely enough, my mother and father did.*
Clergyman:	*Now, you should not set these boys a-laughing …..'*

But for Charles it was no laughing matter. The problem was that he was the child of nonconformists and had been baptised as an infant by his grandfather and without sponsors. While the Anglican clergyman also believed in infant baptism there was an important difference. The clergyman argued that according to scripture, repentance and faith are necessary prerequisites to baptism and

> *for this reason we appoint sponsors (god parents). … I had no more right than you to holy baptism, but the promise of my sponsors was accepted by the Church as an equivalent. … As a child cannot at the time have faith, we accept the bond that he will; which promise he fulfils at confirmation, when he takes the bond into his own hands.'*

As the discussion continued, Charles found himself agreeing with his teacher that repentance and faith were necessary before baptism, but disagreeing that sponsors could take vows on behalf of infants. Before the conversation ended Charles had talked himself into a believer's baptism viewpoint, one that he never left thereafter. His parents, nonconformists both, sent their son to an Anglican school and he came out a Baptist by conviction!

In August 1849, fifteen-year-old Charles moved to Newmarket in Cambridgeshire to become a pupil-teacher in a school there. He both studied under the headmaster, John Swindell, and taught the younger children. Charles continued to be an avid reader and even at that young age the books he most appreciated were those written by the Puritans. While what he read made a great impression on him, it was the school cook who gave him what he called his first lessons in theology. Mary King was 'a good old soul' who 'lived strongly as well as fed strongly.' And she certainly dealt in strong matters, for it was with her that Charles thrashed out such subjects as the covenant of grace, the doctrine of election, union with Christ and the hope of heaven. Weighty matters for a school cook and a teenaged boy! When the lad asked why she attended the local church where there was little meat on the bones of the sermon, Mary King replied that she liked to go to worship even if she got nothing from the sermon. 'You see,' she explained, 'a hen scratching all over a heap of rubbish to try to find some corn; she does not get any, but it shows she is looking for it, and using the means to get it, and then, too, the exercise warms her.' The woman's spiritual faculties were warmed by the exercise of trying to find something in the sermons to feed on. And when Charles complained to her of one particular sermon in which he had found nothing at all, she had the perfect answer. 'I got on better tonight, for to all the preacher said, I just put in a "not" and that turned his talk into real Gospel.' So it was that at Newmarket Charles learned the school curriculum served with a healthy balance of sound Christian common sense. And he learned something else too, thanks to the cook, that 'True seekers will hunt everywhere for Jesus, and will not be too proud to learn from beggars and little children. We take gold from dark mines or muddy streams: it were foolish to refuse instruction in salvation from the most unlettered or uncouth.'

Through a Friend's Eyes

A colleague at the school in Newmarket gives us an interesting insight into the young Charles Spurgeon. From him we learn that he had strong Puritanical views, that he was an able student, shrewd, earnest, hardworking and conscientious.

He also enjoyed a good joke. When the two young men walked together Charles was given to repeating to his friend great chunks of open-air sermons that he had heard. When he wasn't preaching second-hand sermons he was regaling him with long passages from books by John Bunyan. 'He was a delightful companion, cheerful and sympathetic; a good listener as well as a good talker. And he was not cast in a common conventional mould, but had a strong character of his own.' That last comment was to be repeated throughout the years of Charles Spurgeon's life for there was something in him that marked him out as different.

As his friend at Newmarket discovered, Charles was not slow to speak about the Christian faith even though he had still to espouse it for himself. He was well-taught because he had been brought up steeped in Christianity. Later he was to argue for Christian education for young people from his memory of his own early understanding. As a child Spurgeon had listened to his grandfather and father discussing theology with their friends and he had taken away from their discussions what he could understand. In fact, he contended that 'children are capable of understanding some things in early life, which we hardly understand afterwards. Children have eminently a simplicity of faith … I know not that there is much distinction between the simplicity of a child and the genius of the profoundest mind.' By the time Charles was fifteen, he was more than able to discuss the deepest doctrines even though his knowledge was still held in his head rather than his heart.

Like many children of ministers Spurgeon was a critical listener. When preachers used phrases like 'As I have already observed' he wondered why things needed to be repeated. If they were good they would hit home the first time and if not they were not worth saying again. The way in which preachers used their voices interested him. Some men droned their way through sermons, prompting from Charles the pithy comment, 'What a pity that a man … should commit ministerial suicide by harping on one string, when the Lord had given him an instrument of many strings to play upon!' There must be many ministers who with their wives have been treated to such comments from their children as the following on a sermon on 'Who passing through the valley of Baca make it a well'. 'Certainly, the preacher did not make his sermon a well, for it was dry as a stick, and not worth hearing.' And it may have irritated the Spurgeons too. Perhaps it would not have done so had they seen their son's comments as part of his own ministerial training in preaching technique, at least in learning how not to do it. But that was still in the future.

As Charles progressed through his sixteenth year he continued to be burdened by a conviction of sin. Having been early aware of the existence of hell, the youth found that was no longer what horrified him. What troubled him most was not the potential eternal consequences of his sin but sin itself. He knew in his heart that he deserved whatever punishment God saw fit to say was his, for he was given a sense of the Lord's holiness that cast such a light on his heart as to make it seem as dark as hell itself. It seemed to Charles that God's honour was at stake, and that he should not be forgiven lightly or unjustly. 'How could God be just, and yet justify me who had been so guilty?' he asked himself. And he could find no answer. The truth is that Charles' heart was blind to the truth that his mind knew so well, as blind, he contended, as if he had been 'born and bred a heathen.' The young Charles Spurgeon had been brought up with praying for forgiveness as much part of his life as cleaning his teeth, but it was only when he considered the holiness of God and the utter loathsomeness of his sin that he saw himself 'standing before God, in the immediate presence of the heart-searching Jehovah' and the only sentence he could say was, 'God be merciful to me, a sinner.' For such a young man he carried a heavy consciousness of sin. Despite his prayers relief did not come, for he believed himself to be so unworthy that divine justice would not allow an answer, that however earnestly he cried to God his prayer would not penetrate heaven because of its presumptuousness.

What kind of young man was Charles Spurgeon? Although he was most acutely aware of the sinfulness of his heart, he did admit, 'Sometimes, when I began to take stock of myself, I really thought I was quite a respectable lad, and might have been half inclined to boast that I was not like other boys – untruthful, dishonest, disobedient, swearing, Sabbath-breaking, and so on.' That gives us a clearer picture. What we have is a young man who led an outwardly upright life but who was aware of the sinfulness of his heart. And it was Moses who brought that awareness, for when Charles thought of the ten commandments God gave to Moses they all seemed to join in accusing and condemning him in the sight of the most holy God. Years later Spurgeon thought back to his pre-conversion days and thanked God that when he most desired to sin the opportunity was often not there, and when the opportunity was there the desire was not.

For months Charles continued in this state, but he knew where to go for help for he went to his Bible, even though the state of his mind and heart coloured what he read. 'The threatenings were all printed in capitals, but the promises were in such small type I could not for a long time make them out; and when I did read them, I did not believe they were mine; but the threatenings were all my own.' Then, in his anguish of soul, Charles had an experience he was never to forget. His upbringing meant that he had never really been an unbeliever, in that he had always believed that God was. But suddenly the thought insinuated itself into his mind that God didn't exist at all, that there was no heaven and no hell, and that his prayers were just words that disappeared in the air. For a brief period he felt liberated for he was no longer aware of the burden of sin. What, after all, was sin if there was no God to be offended? Doubting everything he had ever been taught was one thing, but when Satan tempted Charles to doubt his very existence he overstretched his hand. 'The very extravagance of the doubt proved its absurdity,' he said. How long this assault lasted is not known, but even if it was short-lived it was desperately powerful. Summing it up, Spurgeon said, 'Whatever staggering doubt, or hideous blasphemy, or ghastly insinuations, even of suicide itself, may assail my feeble heart, they cannot outdo the horror of great darkness through which my spirit passed when I was struggling after a Saviour.'

Broken Resolutions

Desperate to settle the matter, Charles turned to desperate measures. Even though he knew from his childhood that salvation was all of God, and that no matter how much anyone did they could not earn a place in heaven, he made resolution after resolution and broke them all. Later he compared his frenzy of effort to Adam and Eve hurriedly sewing aprons out of fig leaves in order to escape the all-seeing eye of God! As he listened to sermons week after week he longed for preachers to tell him what to do to be saved, as if he were able to do anything. He just could not grasp the fact that Christ had done all on the cross. What a lot he still had to learn, but Christ was his teacher. First he was shown that all his good works could achieve nothing, and Charles felt he had reached rock bottom. But he had further still to go before he was truly brought to see the corruption of his heart and the fact that he could do nothing whatever about it. It was then that he saw in his mind's eye the Lord Jesus on the cross. Looking up at the Lord he recognised that he, Charles Spurgeon, was at one with Christ's enemies who surrounded the cross and he knew then for a certainty that he had no saving faith.

The young Spurgeon went through great traumas in his search for peace, and we have to remember as we read the account of his struggles that they took place over a short space of time because when we reach the most momentous event of his life he was still just fifteen years old. It was Sunday 6th January 1850, and snowing hard in Colchester. Charles was up early to read his Bible and pray, but his quiet time brought him no peace. On his mother's recommendation he set out to hear a certain preacher, but the snow fell so heavily that he took refuge in the Primitive Methodist Church in Artillery Street rather than go any further. Only fifteen people had braved the storm to attend and the preacher did not arrive. Presumably the weather had got the better of him too. A thin man, 'with no pretence to education' took the pulpit instead. No doubt Charles thought little of him to start with because he stumbled over his words as he read from the Bible. Then he took for his text 'Look unto Me, and be ye saved, all the ends of the earth' (Is. 45:22 KJV). Charles sat back to listen to what the man had to say.

Eleven years later Spurgeon, whose memory was quite remarkable, quoted that unlearned sermon in a sermon of his own. Let him tell of his life-changing experience just as it happened. 'He read his text. It was as much as he could do. The text was, "Look to Me, and be saved, all the ends of the earth." He was an ignorant man, he could not say much; he was obliged to keep to his text. Thank God for that. He began, "Look, that is not hard work. You need not lift your hand, you do not want to lift your finger. Look, a fool can do it. It does not need a wise man to look. A child can do that. You don't need to be full-grown to use your eyes. Look, a poor man may do that, no need of riches to look. Look, how simple." Then he went on: "Look unto Me. Do not look to yourselves, but look to Me, that is Christ. Do not look to God the Father to know whether you are elected or not, you shall find that out afterwards; look to Me, look to Christ. Do not look to God the Holy Spirit to know whether he has called you or not; that you shall discover by and by. Look unto Jesus Christ." And then he went on to put it in his simple way thus, "Look unto Me; I am sweating great drops of blood for you; look unto Me, I am scourged and spit upon; I am nailed to the cross, I die, I am buried, I rise and ascend, I am pleading before the Father's throne, and all this is for you.'

It is little wonder that Charles Spurgeon's young heart was moved by the simplicity and force of the sermon. But more was to come. 'Young man, you are very miserable,' the preacher said, looking directly at Charles. And there could have been no doubt who was being spoken to for there were only fourteen others in the building and not many of them would be young men. 'So was I,' the preacher went on, speaking to Spurgeon directly. 'And you will always be miserable if you don't do as my text tells you, and that is Look to Christ.' Then raising his voice to its limit, he called out, 'Young man, look! In God's name, look! And look now. Look! Look! Look! You have nothing to do but look and live.' That was probably the most unlearned sermon Charles Spurgeon had ever heard. It might have been the emptiest church he had ever sat it. He was probably as uncomfortable as he had ever been in church, soaked through with melting snow. But a transaction took place between him and Almighty God because Charles did look to Jesus and was taken from the despair of his heart into 'fullness of joy and hope.' He had left home at 10.30 that morning a sinner oppressed by the weight of his sinfulness, and as he walked home less than two hours later his heart was so joyful it wanted to make his legs dance! He must have felt once again like the fifteen-year-old he was.

Believers' Baptism

What rejoicing there would have been in the Spurgeon home that night when Charles told his parents of his conversion. Many years of prayers had been answered. No wonder it was late into the night before John and his son finished talking and went to bed. The Christmas holiday was soon over and Charles returned to his pupil teaching post at Newmarket. He was hardly back when the subject of believers' baptism came into his mind and before long he wrote to his father explaining his position and asking permission to be baptised. Charles also wrote to his mother. John's reply was guarded though he did not forbid believers' baptism. On 3rd May 1850 Spurgeon was baptised in the River Lark along with two others. Discussing the subject with his mother, she admitted, that though she had often prayed for the Lord to make her son a Christian, she never asked that he might be a Baptist. With his usual speed of thought, Charles replied, 'Ah, Mother! The Lord has answered your prayer with his usual bounty, and given exceedingly abundantly above what you asked or thought.'

What a lot Charles Spurgeon crammed into the first sixteen years of his life, and the pace was not about to slow down. From pupil teacher in Newmarket to one of the best-known preachers in the world in just a few years sums up what followed, though it does need to be unpacked. Twenty months after his conversion, and with no formal theological training at all, Charles took on the pastorate of Waterbeach Baptist Chapel near Cambridge. Around forty people gathered in the little thatched building when he arrived. Two years later the attendance averaged 400. This was not all to do with Spurgeon's preaching, though he was undoubtedly popular and gifted, for these two years coincided with a time of spiritual awakening in the area. Having said that, it was a quite remarkable start to his ministry. In late 1853 Charles accepted an invitation to preach in New Park Street Chapel in London, despite the fact that he was still not twenty years old. His age made him hesitate to move there, but the congregation was so united in their wish to have him as their pastor that he did. Thus began what was probably London's most remarkable ministry. Within two years, interest in his sermons was so widespread that they were published weekly and posted as far away as America.

Before long New Park Street Chapel was too small to hold the crowds that wanted to attend services even though it held 2000 people, 500 of whom stood throughout the services. Until a more suitable building could be constructed the congregation moved first to the Exeter Hall, then to the Surrey Music Hall. Spurgeon's popularity with the many thousands who came to hear his preaching bred unpopularity with others who said that the 'boy preacher' was a performing upstart. When accused of being theatrical and vulgar he said that if he was either of these things it was not intentional, but that his calling was to make people listen to what he said.

He was certainly an odd sight in the pulpit when he first went to London, and we know that from none other than his wife Susanna. When she saw him initially she could hardly believe her eyes. Instead of the usual formal tailor-made suit, the young preacher wore a rough suit that looked as though it had been made by a village seamstress. It was topped by a black satin collar and, most remarkably, a large blue and white spotted handkerchief! Although Spurgeon's appearance that day made a negative impression on the young woman it obviously did not last as they were married in 1856. Their marriage was blessed with twin sons, Charles and Thomas, both of whom became Baptist ministers. The sadness of their married life was that for much of the time Susanna was an invalid, although she had a remarkable book distribution ministry from the confines of their home.

Two things marked the four years that the congregation met in the Surrey Hall. On 19th October 1853, the first occasion they held an evening service there, the place was packed and thousands stood outside hoping to get in. Someone inside the building, it is thought maliciously, shouted that there was a fire. In the rush to get out seven people were crushed to death and many others injured. Spurgeon's enemies saw that as judgement and the press tore his reputation to shreds. But the other thing that marked the congregation's stay in the Surrey Hall was a quite remarkable growth in attendance. The minister was able to say of that period, and of the five years that followed it, 'There has not been a single day but what I have heard of two, three or four having been converted.' Spurgeon's enemies within London churches may have vilified him partly through jealousy for no other congregation grew as his did. Or they may have reasoned that in order to be so popular Spurgeon was not preaching the true gospel, including the offence of the cross. Had they but read his printed sermons they would have discovered that he did indeed preach the whole counsel of God. The truth is that Charles Spurgeon preached God's Word, perhaps in a rather unconventional way, and the Holy Spirit blessed it remarkably. In 1859 the Metropolitan Tabernacle opened with a capacity of almost 6,000 and it was to that number of people Spurgeon preached each week from then until his death over thirty years later.

A Big-Hearted Man

Although Charles is perhaps best remembered as a preacher, that was not all that he did for the Lord. Having had no formal theological training himself he set up the Pastor's College to train men as preachers, especially those whose limited schooling would not have been accepted elsewhere. His two-year course was comprehensive and almost 1,000 men benefited from it in his lifetime. Letters to My Students is a collection of his Friday discourses in the Pastor's College. Spurgeon also had a heart for children and he was instrumental in setting up the Stockwell Orphanages, one for boys and one for girls. The beginning of his ministry in London coincided with an outbreak of cholera that left many orphans in the city and he never forgot their desperate plight. When money was made available in 1867 he used it to open the boys' orphanage and the girls' one followed a short time later. The Metropolitan Tabernacle, under Spurgeon's guidance, supported mission work of many kinds, almshouses for the poor, and the sale of Christian books. It has to be said that books played a huge part in Charles Spurgeon's life because he wrote well over a hundred.

As a boy Charles pressed a great deal of living into his life. His ministry was also marked by great busyness so that when he died, aged just fifty-seven, the space he left seemed enormous. People all over the world mourned his loss and missed his weekly printed sermons. Londoners lost a man who loved them with a passion second only to his love of the Lord. Hundreds of thousands grieved a preacher whose sermons blessed them. Hundreds, no doubt, were not sorry about his passing, as he had been a thorn in their flesh throughout his ministry. And 14,692 people who had become members of his churches must have thought back to the day when he helped them to take their stand for the King of kings and Lord of lords.

Charles Spurgeon was born again when he was just fifteen years old, but the depth and breadth of his spiritual experience before his conversion was quite remarkable, and it gave him an extraordinary degree of insight into the minds of those to whom he preached in later years. From his early childhood in his grandparent's home he had a fear of the last judgement, a fear that lent passion to his preaching at the thought that there were those listening to him who might never again have the opportunity to hear the gospel. It is clear from Charles's description of his farewell to his grandfather when he was leaving Stambourne that these two were not afraid to show their emotions. At a time when emotions were often very firmly buttoned up, Spurgeon went on to be an emotional preacher. He saw emotion as a God-given gift, and if it could be used to help towards the conversion of a lost soul then so much the better. Emotion of a different sort made a huge impression on the young Charles when his mother had her family round the table on Sunday evenings. It is hard to imagine what it would be like to hear your mother praying that she would have to witness against her children in the last day if they had not come to faith because they had been given the opportunity to do so. The awful seriousness of that thought stayed with him, and became part of his ministry.

Throughout his unconverted years Spurgeon attended church, and he was a critical listener. However, his criticisms were redeemed when they effectively became part of his training for the ministry, albeit sometimes on a 'how not to do it' basis. Richard Knill's prophecy that Charles would preach in the biggest church in the country does not seem to have made him personally ambitious, as can be seen by his reticence to move to London from his first church. That lack of personal ambition along with his humility remained with Charles throughout the years when he was London's most popular preacher. Criticism could affect him deeply, and at times when that was the case, his wife was God's instrument of healing.

7

Isobel Kuhn

Isobel and John Kuhn served the Lord as missionaries to the Lisu people in China and Thailand, and the books she wrote about their work were popular reading for missionary-minded Christians in the third quarter of the 20th Century. But her first book, By Searching, in which Isobel described how she came to faith was probably the book that spoke most deeply to its readers. The stories she wrote about describing their work were fascinating and exotic to the Western mind, but By Searching described what was familiar and personal, for it was an account of her own spiritual journey before coming to faith and the struggles she had in her early Christian life. Other books have overtaken Isobel Kuhn's with the passage of the years, but they still have lessons to teach us. The raw honesty of her testimony in By Searching is as fresh as when it was written in 1957.

Born Isobel Miller, she was the daughter of Sam and Alice, a Canadian Christian couple. Her father was an elder and keen lay preacher in a Presbyterian church and her grandfather was a Presbyterian minister. Isobel's home was one in which Christ was often spoken about, and discussions about the Christian faith were held without embarrassment. The Millers were interested not only in their local church but in the work of the gospel worldwide, and missionaries were often among those who were welcomed as guests in their home. Personal piety was encouraged, and Isobel and her brother were brought up to read their Bibles and pray as well as attend church services. They would have no more thought of missing church on a Sunday than of missing school on a Monday morning. It was part and parcel of their family life.

An able and conscientious girl, Isobel worked hard at school and acquitted herself well. It looked as though she would have no problem achieving her long-held ambition to be a schoolteacher. She was also musically gifted, taking that from her mother who had given up a promising professional career as a pianist to bring up her young family. As the time drew near for his daughter to move from school to university, her father made it his business to prepare Isobel for the kind of thinking she would meet there. Having been taught to accept the Bible as the true and inerrant Word of God, he explained that she would meet among her contemporaries and teachers some who took a much more liberal view. They saw Jesus as a teacher and example rather than a saviour, and the Bible as an interesting historical document rather than the one and only rule of faith and life. Some, he told her, discarded God's Word altogether, and he warned against coming under their influence.

Signed the Pledge

The environment in which Isobel and her brother were reared was strictly teetotal, and children in the church were encouraged, when they were so young that alcohol was not a temptation, to make a decision never to drink. When she was twelve years of age, Isobel and several of her friends 'signed the pledge' never to let alcohol pass their lips. Before she started university her father, a medical man, reminded her of the effect that alcohol could have on a girl, and told her in graphic detail some of the problems young women, who had made unwise decisions while under the influence of alcohol, brought into his consulting room. Full of good advice from every direction Isobel embarked on her university career expecting to come out the other end of it as a Christian and a teacher. Known as a believer among her school friends, she was prepared to stand up for her faith in university too. But it did not take long for her approach to be challenged, and when the challenge came Isobel Miller was quite unprepared to meet it.

'Of course no-one in this enlightened age believes any more in the myths of Genesis …' her lecturer said, looking round the lecture hall full of first-year-students. Most looked comfortable with his assertion, but a few squirmed and he knew it. Deciding to put them to the test he went on, 'Is there anyone here who believes there is a heaven and a hell, who believes that the story of Genesis is true?' He asked for hands to be raised. Only two hands went up out of the class of around a hundred. Smiling condescendingly, the lecturer told the pair of them, Isobel Miller and one other, that they only believed because their parents had told them to. Then he continued with his lecture. Isobel was in turns embarrassed and upset and outraged. How dare he insinuate that her faith was second-hand rather than real and personal! How dare he make it sound as if nobody in their right mind believed the Bible in the 20th Century! But as she walked home later that afternoon her mind played with the subject. Isobel, who was a young woman of intellectual integrity, asked herself if her lecturer's accusation was true. Did she only believe the Bible because those who meant most to her, and whom she loved and trusted, had taught her it was true? She could not remember a time when she had not believed. But did that make it true? What objective test could she apply to prove the existence of God and his involvement in the world, not to mention Jesus' saving death and resurrection? Seeing herself as a modern young woman she decided to apply modern scientific investigative procedures to the problem. If God existed then she would prove he existed, and until she was able to prove his existence she would assume that there was no God. She was uncomfortable about just one thing, the memory of occasions in her family's life when she had seen prayers answered. But in the short time since she had started her journey home from university that day Isobel had travelled a long distance. Thinking about the matter briefly she dismissed answered prayer as invalid proof of God's existence. After all, she reasoned, mind has a powerful effect over matter. She knew that from her study of psychology. Perhaps she had willed things to happen rather than God making them happen. Isobel Miller made a decision. She would accept no theory of life which she had not proved personally. That felt good. It felt liberating.

The following morning felt good too, for there was no reason to be up early to read her Bible and pray before going to university. The absurdity of prayer struck her forcibly. All these years she had been speaking to 'someone' who perhaps did not exist, let alone hear her speaking. She was almost embarrassed at the thought of it, though the whole business of prayers she had apparently seen answered was the only part of her new freedom that troubled her slightly. One thing Isobel could not brush off as easily as Bible reading and prayer was the effect of the name of Jesus. Having been brought up to love the Lord Jesus it was not as easy to shrug him off as it was to abandon the trappings of religion. Despite that she 'broke with the old religious habits and frankly went into the world.' In their confusion and distress at this turn of events, it must have been a comfort to her parents that Isobel had a fastidious nature and neither smoked nor drank. But instead of being involved in church weeknight activities, her time was now taken up with amateur acting and dancing. In 1922 the comment beside her picture in her university yearbook read, 'And oh the tilt of her heels when she dances!' For all that her life had changed, Isobel was still viewed as a Christian by her fellow students. But she knew she was not. Neither was she an atheist; she was keeping her mind too honestly open to use that description of herself. Rather she was an agnostic seeking for truth. Recognising that her daughter had not closed her mind completely, Alice Miller persuaded her to go along to meetings at the

Young Women's Christian Association. Politeness took Isobel there a few times but boredom set in and she did not go back. That too was liberating as it gave a sense of freedom from her mother as well as from religion.

During her second year at university, when Isobel was more than ever under the influence of her lecturer's materialistic thinking, she was involved with a young man to whom she became secretly engaged. He, like her, was from a Christian home, but although she sometimes went to church with him – 'it made a nice, inexpensive date' – their behaviour was 'perceptibly down-grade.' If a young woman Isobel's age made that comment today it would be assumed that she and her boyfriend were involved in a physical relationship, but from what she wrote later in her life it is clear that was not the case. Her fastidiousness would not have allowed it. For the first time in her life Isobel Miller ran with the crowd, and she enjoyed it. Without Christian constraints she could relax instead of wondering if Jesus would approve of the company she kept and the things they did.

One Freedom too Far

Isobel's enjoyment of her new-found freedom was short-lived, because her 'fiancé' felt more liberated than she did, quite liberated enough to date another girl while he was unofficially engaged to her. Never did freedom seem such a bitter pill as it did to Isobel when she heard the news. Alice Miller, who was quite a domineering woman, was so full of advice that her daughter could take none of it. But her father was different. He understood Isobel better and they were very close. Also, as he was a doctor, he recognised the signs of distress and sleeplessness that her heartbreak caused. One night, as she lay tossing and turning in bed, she heard the doorhandle turn. Closing her eyes she pretended to be asleep. Whether her father was aware that Isobel was awake or not, he knelt at the side of her bed and prayed for her. 'Thanks, Dad,' she said, opening her eyes. 'I know you mean it well, but it doesn't go beyond the ceiling, you know.' Rising to his feet, her father groaned in deep distress at what had been said and left the room.

A short time later, around the time of Isobel's twentieth birthday, she reached a crisis point. Unable to sleep, her broken romance going round and round in her mind, she decided that her former fiancé was just an average man, and probably all average men two-timed their girls. The thought of sharing the one she loved revolted her and if she could not have him to herself then, she decided, life was pointless, futile. That probably started off as a throwaway thought, but the devil encouraged her to think on the matter and before long Isobel was seriously considering taking her own life. There was, she knew, a bottle marked 'poison' in the bathroom. All she had to do was drink it. But as she grasped her bedroom door handle her father groaned deeply in his sleep three times. Suddenly she realised what she was going to inflict on him. If she committed suicide he would think she was in hell, because he believed in hell and knew she was not yet a Christian. The young woman couldn't think straight. There is no hell, she told herself, but Dad believes there is and he'll think that's where I've gone. Her resolve to take her life crumpled at the thought of what it would do to her much-loved father. She did not choose to live rather than die by her own hand; she chose to live rather than break his heart. Sitting on the edge of her bed she felt more miserable than she had ever thought possible.

As she sat there Isobel remembered a quotation from Dante, a favourite of the lecturer who had undermined her faith in the first place. The quotation was in Italian: In la sua volontade e nostra pace, which she translated as In his will is our peace. It seemed almost as though the words lit up the darkness of her room as she realised that Dante had believed in God. How else could he have written, 'In his will is our peace'? Raising both hands above her head, Isobel whispered a prayer not knowing if there was anyone there to hear it. 'God, if there be a God, if you will prove to me that you are, and if you will give me peace, I will give you my whole life. I'll do anything you ask me to do, go where you send me, obey you all my days.' With her emotions torn to shreds, Isobel lay down, pulled the covers over herself and waited for another sleepless night. Opening her eyes what seemed like minutes later, she realised that her bedroom was bathed in December morning sunlight! It took Isobel a little time to remember what had happened in the middle of the night. Then her heart told her that she had made a bargain with God if he would give her the gift of peace, and he had. But her mind argued that it was mind over matter. All that had happened was that she'd passed on her problems to an imaginary god and so relieved herself of them.

Secret Search

Isobel Miller was an honest young woman. She knew that she'd made a bargain and she tried to work out what it meant in practice. How was she to seek God? Where should she begin? As she puzzled over it a picture came into her mind from a conference she had attended the previous summer. A young man (she had written him off as a fundamentalist) spoke of his internment in Germany during the 1914-18 war. 'While I was interned in Germany as a prisoner of war,' he said, 'I got hold of a Bible and started to read it. I found God through reading his Word.' She could not remember the speaker's name but Isobel could picture his radiant face. She blew the dust off her Bible and wondered where to begin reading. Immediately her scepticism kicked in. Moses didn't write the Pentateuch, she thought, so there's no point in beginning at Genesis. Had any part of the Bible been proved to be true? she wondered. Then she realised that as the historicity of Jesus was beyond doubt she should begin reading his life story in the gospels. She decided that she would read only the gospels, no other parts of the Bible at all, and that she would mark everything Jesus said we should do, and then she would do them. As Jesus prayed she decided to start praying again, although still not knowing if there was anyone there to whom she was praying. And all that before breakfast!

For the three months that followed, Isobel's outward life showed no sign of change at all, quite deliberately. Her search for God was carried out in secret. Consequently although she studied the gospel carefully and critically she did not attend church or ask any others about the faith. Some time into her investigation – because that was how she was treating it – she was snubbed by her former boyfriend at a dance, something that upset her deeply. Dashing into the privacy of a bedroom she prayed for calmness, and was suddenly quiet and poised. By the end of the evening she was bursting with pride at how she had coped. But later, when once again she couldn't sleep, even Isobel Miller knew that was not mind over matter because she knew her own mind. She had prayed for help and God had helped her. That experience convinced her of the existence of God, but only in terms of being a prayer-answering power to which she now had access. Before she fell asleep she found herself making a wish-list of things she wanted and that she could now have through prayer. In the months that followed it seemed that God was just pandering to her selfishness. She prayed for invitations to dances and they came in the most unlikely ways. Isobel prayed all kinds of selfish and self-indulgent prayers and God heard and answered. But, as she wrote later of that time in her life, 'Follow me in my pursuit of God – yes. Like me, come to him via the Christ of Calvary – yes. Seek for the revelation of that Christ in the Bible – yes. But don't imitate me in my flounderings. I was pigheaded now in the matter of refusing all human advice, and my own level of living was so low that God could not meet me on a higher ... I am sure God gave (these answers to selfish prayers) to me. Moreover, by piling on the triumphs he taught me a lesson I never forgot. I learned that pride and vanity could never bring me peace or happiness. ... I was miserable.'

Although Isobel continued to sleep on Sundays rather than go to church, her parents discerned a slight softening in her attitude. Alice Miller grasped the nettle and asked her daughter if she would attend a meeting with her, assuring her that it was a class in a Bible school, not in church. Isobel rather surprised herself by agreeing to go. Ignoring the audience completely, she began to listen to what she expected to be a boring talk. It was not. The speaker, taking as his subject the temptations of Christ, discussed the liberal interpretation of the passage, then 'without any belligerent dogmatism, he courteously but deftly refuted their arguments.' Isobel 'saw clearly that here was a scholar who knew both sides of the argument. Here was a real gentleman who would never stoop to nasty remarks about an opponent. And, watching the quiet radiance of his face, (she) instinctively knew that here was a man who had a personal experience with God.' Having decided to attend his next lecture, Isobel turned round to look at the rest of the audience. An elderly man, a friend of her father, was sitting right behind. His greeting stunned her for he told the young woman that he had been praying for her for the last seven years. She tried to thank him, then left as soon as she could. Seven years took her back to when she first began to turn her back on her childhood faith. The following Sunday saw her back in church.

In May 1922 Isobel graduated, and nine months later she began her teaching career in Cecil Rhodes School, Vancouver, with a class of eight-year-olds. Her aim was to teach English and become a university dean of women, but she had to start at the bottom of the ladder. As her family moved to Victoria, BC, she had for the first time to live away from home. The boarding house in which she lived was home to a number of young people, none of whom attended church. It is interesting to note one short sentence in her account of that time. 'So I found myself in this house – the only Christian.' As that was written thirty five years after the event, by which time she was a missionary of long experience, we take Isobel at her word that she was then a Christian. But she was a very small child in the faith, one who had a lot of stumbling to do before she began to walk. In fact, had she not made that statement, someone reading her life story might have put her conversion at a later date. God deals with people differently. Some accounts in this book have shown instant life changes at conversion. Others, like Isobel Miller, take longer to find their feet. It is instructive, therefore, to follow her through the next phase of her life.

Times Tables

Teaching was a terrible disappointment and discipline a real problem. Isobel loved the children but the subjects bored her. Because she could not raise any enthusiasm for the kind of things eight-year-olds need to be taught, they weren't enthusiastic either. Spelling, times tables and drill did nothing for either the pupils or their young teacher. It does not put it too strongly to say that Isobel hated her job. Afraid of failure, she signed up for a convention she thought would help. It was to be held in Seattle and she arranged to meet up with a boy she knew there. Isobel was less than pleased when a telegram arrived from her father telling her that he had arranged for her to stay with a friend of his! All she remembered about the Whipples was that they were religious friends of her parents, and that was just what she did not want.

To Isobel's relief she discovered that Mrs Whipple was not a religious fanatic whose one aim was to pin her down and thrash her with the gospel. Instead she was a cultured, gentle and motherly woman who welcomed the young teacher to her heart as well as her home. In fact, during their first day together God was not even mentioned. What Isobel did not know was that when she went to bed that night Mrs Whipple got down on her knees and prayed for over an hour for her guest. Having done that she went to bed knowing her friends' daughter was in God's good hands. The following day Isobel attended church with the Whipples, then she visited a friend. Admitting that she was miserable in her job, Isobel was very open to her friend's suggestion that she consult a phrenologist who happened to be visiting her parents. The idea of having the bumps on her head read and her future told appealed greatly to the worried young teacher, but respect for her hostess held her back. She told her friend that she would call her after speaking to Mrs Whipple. Interestingly, it didn't occur to Isobel that the gracious woman would object to her becoming involved in this very suspect occult cum pseudoscientific practice, just that she might not want her to consult the phrenologist on a Sunday!

When Isobel returned to her hostess's home she asked outright if Mrs Whipple would mind her having her head read. Quite unfazed by the question, the wise woman suggested they discuss the matter, and that another guest – also a school teacher – might join in the discussion. Leaving her two visitors together briefly Mrs Whipple gathered her daughter and two teenaged friends and asked them to pray as they discussed phrenology. Leaving them to do that, she returned to her guests and gently invited Isobel to explain the situation. With these comfortable middle-aged women she felt able to pour out her sadness, disappointment and feelings of failure. Then she went on to say what a wonderful opportunity it was to be able to consult the phrenologist who would point her in the right direction for her life.

God's Plan

Mrs Whipple had won Isobel's trust and confidence and she felt able to say what was she was thinking, knowing that the three youngsters were praying for her to say the right thing. Her words made such an impression on Isobel Miller that she quoted them in By Searching. 'I don't think the matter of its being Sunday is the important thing,' Mrs Whipple said. 'It's like this: God has a plan for your life. The Bible says that he has created us unto good works and foreordained that we should walk in them. That means he has foreordained a useful life for you, and he does so for all of his creatures. The point as I see it is – to find out God's plan for your life and then follow it. If it is his will to reveal that plan through a phrenologist, going on Sunday would do no harm. But if it were not his will to reveal his plan through a phrenologist, going any day of the week would be wrong.' Although she had been brought up in a Christian home, this sounded like news to the young woman. She could not remember being told that God had a plan for her life, but it may be that she just had not listened. The idea that God was intimately interested in her, that he would plan a life especially for her, touched her to 'breaking point'. Struggling to control herself, Isobel asked how she could find out what his plan was.

Mrs Whipple, still avoiding abusing her relationship with Isobel by preaching to her vulnerability, just said that she had always found God's will through the Bible, adding that whatever his plan was it would always be in accordance with the Bible. Just then the telephone rang. Not ignoring it because she thought she was making headway in her argument, Mrs Whipple left the room, leaving the two schoolteachers to continue their talk. If God's plan for me is in the Bible, what does it have to say about phrenology? Isobel wondered. Opening the book quite at random she laid her hand on the open page and read the words to which she was pointing. 'Keep thee far from a false matter' (Ex. 23:7). A surge of relief pulsed through the young woman. Suddenly it made sense that God had a plan for her life for he obviously had a message to her immediate question. Phrenology was not his way to help her out of her present difficulty. Utterly exhausted, Isobel wept her heart out to the two older women. Even then, Isobel wrote, 'Mrs Whipple never tried to pry; the privacy of the human soul was respected by her, and that was another reason we all loved and trusted her so.' What a lesson to those in whom others confide.

Before Isabel left to return to Vancouver, Mrs Whipple told her about The Firs Bible Conference and asked her to attend as her guest. That did not seem possible as the young woman had applied to attend a teaching course that she thought might help her work situation. Before the conference was due to take place Mrs Whipple sent her young friend enough money for the fare should she change her mind, and she did. The Firs (as it was called) was to have a profound effect on the muddled young Christian that Isobel Miller was. In By Searching she wrote that Mrs Whipple, 'saw, as I had not, that here was one groping blindly toward God, and open to dangerous misleading if not carefully grounded in the Word. As is a young person's weakness, I might be carried off my feet by some magnetic personality of one of the many "isms", if I chanced to meet such, at this stage. I needed grounding in the Scriptures and I needed

Christian fellowship.' Although Isobel was a Christian, and the product of a Christian home, she was apparently easily led, something that the discerning Mrs Whipple recognised. Not only that, but the lodgings in which she was living were not conducive to growth in the faith, surrounded as she was by card parties, social drinking and late night noise. Also Isobel had starved herself of Christian company by cutting herself off from believers during her years of searching in order that she could discover the truth straight from the gospels rather than be influenced by what other people thought. Consequently, she was not only a young and very immature Christian, she was starved so long of those things that build Christians up that she was unaware of the lack of them. She needed a regular quiet time and the blessing of fellowship with other believers. In fact, she needed The Firs.

Only one space was left at The Firs and it meant sharing a cabin with Mrs Whipple's sister-in-law Edna, a recently-widowed young missionary. She was one of the speakers at the conference, but Isobel wrote of her contact with her, 'Cabin life with her was my first encounter with a Spirit-filled life living in its daily routine habits. It was Edna off the platform who wrought most for me. She sought the Lord's face before that of anyone else's at the beginning of each day. This deeply bruised heart hungered and panted after the Lord, and her first waking thought was a longing for his fellowship and presence. And she kindled the same hunger in me. Remember, I had a bruised heart, too.'

After returning home from The Firs Bible Conference Isobel had to do some very hard thinking, the same thinking that faces every new Christian. What in her life and practice was acceptable to the Lord and what should be jettisoned because it is not appropriate behaviour? The issues for Isobel may seem a little dated today but the principles remain. 'It will astonish some adult readers (and perhaps make them shake their heads dubiously) to learn that all this time I was still indulging in theatres, dances and worldly things,' she wrote.

> 'My father had long years before urged me to separate myself from these amusements, but my mother felt he was "narrow" in his views on such matters, and she felt they did no harm if discriminately chosen. So I had gone with her viewpoint as the easier and more pleasant.'

There had been times when Isobel's young Christian conscience had troubled her a little about some of her activities, but she had always fallen back on her escape clause – 'you are only not doing that because your dad told you not to.' But the time had come when she had to think these things through for herself, and quickly.

The young people in her lodgings often played cards late into the night and Isobel enjoyed playing with them. Suddenly that seemed a waste of time, not to mention a waste of the small sum of money she often lost at the card table. Another big issue for her was her love of long romantic novels, read as an escape from the real world. She especially enjoyed going to bed with one of her books, one that she could not put down until she read to the very last page. Having closed the book in the early hours of the morning Isobel took up her Bible to read it before going to sleep. Over time she discerned that when she did that her appetite for Bible reading diminished. One day it was as though God asked her a strange question. 'When a child fills its stomach with ice-cream and soda-water, why does it lose its appetite for meat and potatoes?' Isobel knew then that it was because she was filling her mind with romantic frivolities that her Bible reading was dry. Did she miss her light novels? Her answer is lovely. 'Does one begrudge candle-light when morning sunshine is pouring in the window? I was richly repaid for this self-discipline.

Awake in the Night

Having seen her friend Edna's desire for daily quiet times with God, Isobel found a growing yearning within herself for the same. But that presented a practical problem because it was hard to organize an evening quiet time when the others in the house were dancing in the next room or playing a noisy game of cards. Mornings were no better because her mind was on teaching as soon as her eyes opened. Isobel made a courageous decision – certainly courageous for her as she was known as a sleepyhead – she asked the Lord to waken her at 2 am, when the house was quiet and peaceful, and to keep her awake and alert for an hour of study and prayer. Those were precious times. It was of those middle of the night quiet times that she was able to say, 'I learned fellowship with Christ, living person-to-person fellowship which henceforth became dearer than ought else in life to me.'

For years, dancing had been a source of enjoyment to Isobel Miller, and she continued to attend dances after The Firs. She would have argued that she was doing nothing wrong, that it was all good clean fun. God used a former friend to teach her that there was another principle at stake in this area of her life. One evening at a dance Isobel met an old university friend. As she knew her friend to be a keen Christian she expressed surprise at seeing her there. The young woman's reply shocked and wounded. 'You're the reason I am here tonight,' her friend said. 'You are a Christian too, aren't you? All through our four years (at university) you danced and had a good time and I got left out of everything. People say you are a good Christian, but you dance, so I decided to dance, too. This is my first dance.' Isobel had already learned that there was right and wrong, but she still had to discover that one Christian's behaviour can drag another down, and that sometimes believers have to stop doing things they enjoy in order not to encourage others into a course of action that might prove unhelpful in the long run.

A short time later Mrs Whipple visited Vancouver and phoned her young friend. Isobel was delighted to see her again, and before long the subject of dancing came up. The older woman gently pointed out that 'all things are lawful to me, but not all things are expedient' (1 Cor. 6:12 KJV). Then she asked a telling question. Had Isobel told anyone she was a Christian? The young schoolteacher was appalled at the thought! 'It is a point of honour among us not to thrust our religious opinions upon the other fellow,' she replied. 'I've never told anyone! It's my private life with God!' Very gently Mrs Whipple led Isobel to discover that as a Christian she had a duty to tell others about the Lord. There seemed such a lot to learn. It is interesting to remember that Isobel Miller was brought up in a Christian home, that her father was a preacher and her grandfather a minister. Yet, it is almost as though she had taken in little or nothing of what went on around her in her growing-up years. Rather than berate her for her ignorance Mrs Whipple gently and positively encouraged her to progress in the life of faith.

When she was invited to the following Firs Bible Conference, Isobel needed no encouragement. The previous year her personal devotional life had been challenged and she had no idea that in 1924 she would meet a challenge of a different sort. One of the speakers was J O Fraser of China Inland Mission. His story held everyone's attention. Fraser had worked for some time near the China / Burma border in the Yunnan Province. As he ministered among the Chinese there, he often noticed traders from a different people group. Their clothes were more colourful and they wore turbans. Although these people know enough Chinese to trade, their language was one the missionary did not know. These were the Lisu people who lived in the mountains on either side of the Salween River canyon. They had not heard of Jesus and their language had never been made into a script. Unlike the Chinese people in the area who worshipped idols, the Lisu were animists, worshipping demons they believed lived in the natural world. Feeling constrained to reach out to these people, J O Fraser and another missionary first learned their language in order to create a written script. His talk each night at The Firs fired Isobel's imagination and something in her began to long to do what the speaker was doing. Having only recently been appalled at the thought of sharing her faith, she now felt the beginnings of a call to do that as her life's work! Mr Fraser concluded his last talk with, 'We need more missionaries – young men of consecration willing for the privations and loneliness such a life entails.' Isobel's 'heart thrilled with love for the Lisu people' and she silently told the Lord that she was willing to go to them – only she wasn't a man!

A Parting and a Meeting

Much to Isobel's surprise her father, who was also at the conference, invited Mr Fraser to spend some time in their family home. Alice Miller was not best pleased as she knew her daughter well enough to recognise the influence such a man might have over her, and she did not intend losing Isobel to missionary work in China, or any other foreign country for that matter. But the young woman did feel God's call to serve him through serving the Lisu people, though her mother died while she was studying at Moody Bible Institute in Chicago and never did have to say goodbye to Isobel as she sailed for China. At Moody she met John Kuhn, to whom the Lord had also given a heart for the Chinese. They were married as young missionaries in their adopted homeland in 1929. It might be thought that Isobel, who had longed to be a missionary in China since hearing Mr Fraser speak at The Firs, would have settled down well when she arrived there five years later, but it was not easy for her. One of the things that had kept her from many temptations in her student years was her fastidiousness. But on arriving in China Isobel discovered that the dust and the noise offended her; not only that but she felt as though she was living in a goldfish bowl. Privacy was a concept the people of China did not seem to understand at all. Everywhere she looked Isobel saw people watching, and the more adventurous touched her to see what fair skin felt like, and they stroked her hair to feel what it was like too. At first these intrusions felt like an assault to Isobel and she had to be reminded by John what God had done for her, and how little a thing a lack of privacy was if it allowed the people around them to learn of the Lord. China Inland Mission, the society with whom they served, did not immediately send them to the China / Burma border to work but to Chengchiang in Yunnan, with the people who live in the Great Plains. By the time they were sent to the Lisu people the Kuhn's had a little daughter, Katherine.

Lights in Lisuland

It was not until March 1930 that John and Isobel exchanged the Great Plains and the Chinese for the mountains of the Upper Salween Canyon and the Lisu people. And they worked with them there and in Thailand, with only a few short interruptions, until 1954. Their son Daniel was born in Lisuland in 1943. China in the 1940s was neither comfortable nor safe. The Second World War that was raging in Europe was the focus of attention and many people did not realise that other parts of the world were also engaged in warfare, China included. The Kuhns, near the border as they were, found themselves threatened on many occasions. For safety's sake young Katherine was sent to Chefoo School in what is now Malaysia. She was not long there when the Japanese captured the school and it was many months before her parents received a letter from her assuring them that she was safe and well. It was so long before the family was reunited that by the time Katherine met her little brother for the first time he was a toddler. Separation was one of the burdens that Isobel had to learn to bear because not only was Katherine away at school, when she was old enough to attend university she went home to Canada. John also travelled in the course of his work and was often absent for long periods of time.

The Kuhns realised that to make the most impact on the Lisu people they had to train new Christians to be leaders and teachers of their own people. That was what inspired the Rainy Season Bible Schools. No doubt Isobel remembered back to the impact The Firs had on her own life and prayed that her Lisu friends would know the same blessing. Rainy Season Bible Schools were well named. During the dry season the Lisu people had to work so hard on the land that there was no time to set aside for study. It was only when the rains came – and when they came they came with a vengeance – that they were able to leave their fields to do the short residential courses the Kuhns and others prepared for them. Because the Lisu people lived in mountainous terrain they risked their lives to attend the Rainy Season Bible Schools, as whole mountainsides could be washed away in a deluge. And weather was not the only problem because Communism was on the march and soldiers were often ruthless. Much of their time with the Lisu people was spent in dangerous situations, but in 1950 things came to a head. Katherine was already in Canada, and it was decided that Isobel and Daniel should join her, leaving John for a time in Lisuland. Mother and son braved snowy mountain passes, bad-tempered border guards, officious soldiers and government red tape before they reached the safety of their ship home. John and Isobel returned to the Lisu people in Thailand in 1951 and served them for a further three years. By then it was clear that Isobel had cancer. She went back home for treatment and spent her final years writing the books that have inspired so much interest in missionary work and in the people of Lisuland. She died in 1957.

When Isobel Kuhn was young, acceptance of the fundamentals of Christianity was being challenged by a new modernism, from which post-modernism has spawned in our own day. She was almost ahead of her time in that post-modernists would concur with her approach to what she had been brought up to believe. It was there not to be accepted but to be challenged. And that's just what she did. Not only that, they would agree with her methodology which was only to believe what she could prove was true, then to believe it only as a personal truth, as other people would find their own version of truth themselves. It took a complete conversion of heart and mind to change her approach, and even then the change was very gradual, instructively so for the student of her life.

When Isobel had dismissed God as nonexistent she experienced a fear that shook her profoundly, driving her to suicide had not her love of her father been so deep. It is interesting that the Lord took her to serve the Lisu people who, in the absence of a belief in a god of any kind, served their demonic fears. If there is no god then this world is a fearful place, as the Lisu people knew only too well. Having 'proved' God experimentally Isobel Kuhn had an opening into the understanding of the people she served. She could understand just a little of the fear they harboured in their hearts and minds and it filled her with a compassion that overrode the very real fear of being a missionary in a war-torn land. God not only redeemed Isobel Kuhn, he redeemed her confusion of thought and helped her to spend her life pointing others in his direction, both in the work she did and through her writing.

Bibliography

The following books were used to research *Gold from Dark Mines*. Some other titles have been added as they will be of interest to anyone wishing to read further on the subjects.

Augustine:
Confessions of St Augustine
The City of God, St Augustine, J M Dent & Sons Ltd, 1931
The Apostle from Africa, David Bentley-Taylor, CFP, 2002
Augustine, Henry Chadwick, OUP, 1986

John Bunyan:
Grace Abounding to the Chief of Sinners, John Bunyan, EP, 2000
John Bunyan, Frank Mott Harrison, Banner of Truth, 1989
Pilgrim and Dreamer, Ernest W Bacon, Paternoster Press, 1983
John Bunyan, John Pestell, Day One, 2002
Pilgrim's Progress, John Bunyan

Selina, The Countess of Huntingdon
Spiritual Pilgrim, Edwin Welch, University of Wales, 1995
Selina, Countess of Huntingdon, Faith Cook, Banner of Truth, 2001

Jonathan Edwards:

Jonathan Edwards, theologian of the heart, Harold Simonson, William B Eerdmans Publishing Company, 1974

Jonathan Edwards, A new biography, Iain H Murray, Banner of Truth, 1987

Memoirs of Jonathan Edwards, Jonathan Edwards

Personal Narrative, Jonathan Edwards

Diary, Jonathan Edwards

Charles H Spurgeon:

The Early Years, Charles H Spurgeon, Banner of Truth, 1976

Spurgeon, Heir of the Puritans, Ernest W Bacon, Allen & Unwin, 1967

The Young Spurgeon, Peter Jeffrey, EP, 1992

Isobel Kuhn:

By Searching, Isobel Kuhn, OMF, 1986

In the Arena, Isobel Kuhn, OMF, 1984

Ascent to the Tribes, Isobel Kuhn, OMF

Green Leaf in Drought, Isobel Kuhn, OMF, 1973

Nests above the Abyss, Isobel Kuhn, OMF, 1983

Precious Things of the lasting Hills, Isobel Kuhn, OMF

Stones of Fire, Isobel Kuhn, OMF

A Heart for Mission

Five Pioneer Thinkers

Ron Davies

Jonathan Edwards, Jan Amos Comenius,
Count Zinzendorf, Cotton Mather, Richard Baxter

The Protestant Missionary effort only really got under way in the late 18th century with the formation of the Baptist Missionary Society. Bearing in mind that the Reformation began in the early 16th Century the obvious question that arises is 'Why did it take Protestants nearly three centuries to act on Jesus' Great Commission mandate?'

This book goes a long way to explain why.

'For those who like to probe beneath the surface of missionary myths – read this fascinating book and be enriched, challenged and inspired.'

Chris Wright
Langham Partnership International

Ron Davies has lectured at All Nations Christian College since 1964 and has been a visiting lecturer at several Seminaries in Eastern Europe and elsewhere.

ISBN 1-85792-233-6

Christian Focus Publications

publishes books for all ages
Our mission statement –

STAYING FAITHFUL

In dependence upon God we seek to help make His infallible Word, the Bible, relevant. Our aim is to ensure that the Lord Jesus Christ is presented as the only hope to obtain forgiveness of sin, live a useful life and look forward to heaven with Him.

REACHING OUT

Christ's last command requires us to reach out to our world with His gospel. We seek to help fulfill that by publishing books that point people towards Jesus and help them develop a Christ-like maturity. We aim to equip all levels of readers for life, work, ministry and mission.

Books in our adult range are published in three imprints.

Christian Focus contains popular works including biographies, commentaries, basic doctrine and Christian living. Our children's books are also published in this imprint.

Mentor focuses on books written at a level suitable for Bible College and seminary students, pastors, and other serious readers. The imprint includes commentaries, doctrinal studies, examination of current issues and church history.

Christian Heritage contains classic writings from the past.

Christian Focus Publications, Ltd.,
Geanies House, Fearn, Ross-shire,
IV20 1TW, Scotland, United Kingdom
info@christianfocus.com
www.christianfocus.com